The Altar of Love

by

Francis Santarose

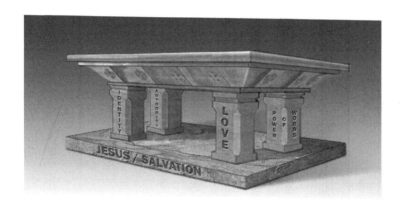

Bulabu Publishing   New Mexico

The Altar of Love

by Francis Santarose

Published in The United States by Bulabu Publishing, New Mexico

Santarose, Francis

Includes Bible references

ISBN: 978-0-9815439-5-6

Printed in the United States of America

About The Author

Francis J. Santarose, an Apostle of God and Servant of Jesus Christ, was called to be a teacher of the Gospel by the Holy Spirit. Santarose, an 8th Don, Grand Master Tae Kwon-Do instructor was saved in 1991, and created a Christian children's ministry called, KID FIT, through his martial arts school, United Tae Kwon-Do, in Houston, Texas. Santarose franchised 22 Christian youth sports camps from 1992 to 2014. He is now a lecturer, Bible teacher, and guest speaker at Encourager Christian Academy, Texas Bible Institute, and Believers World Outreach Men's Retreat. He, also, serves as associate pastor at Christ Over Our Lives Ministries Prison Outreach. In recent years, Santarose has been much sought after for his Holy Spirit guided work to remove demons, illnesses, and brokenness from people who are suffering these afflictions, and restore lasting healing in God's Children.

Preface

I was sitting in the back of this little church one day when the Holy Spirit spoke to me. "I have anointed you with the gift of teaching. Why are you hiding here?" A few weeks later I was still hiding in that little church listening to the pastor preach his sermon. He seemed like a really good pastor. He was very intelligent, well-studied, and a good speaker. He had all the right attributes to preach. As I recall, his sermon seemed like an interesting one at the moment, but when I was driving home, it dawned on me that I could not recall any of what was said that day.

Then, I tried to think of even one of his sermons and I got nothing, nada. How is that possible, I thought? And this is what I heard, "Because it's all fluff to tickle your ears. My sheep need meat. Feed my sheep meat." Later that week, out of the blue, my teenage daughter blurted out, "When are you going to start preaching?"

Interestingly, I was contacted the following week by a church looking for a pastor, but it fell through. Then I was asked if I wanted to use a local business to start my own church, but that fell through. Shortly after, while praying, I asked the Lord, "Clearly you want me to preach, but where?" Immediately, He responded and said, **Where did Jesus preach?** I said, "Everywhere." He said, **Go and do likewise.**

From that moment on, I knew I was not supposed to preach in a brick and mortar building, at least not at that time, but I was to preach everywhere I went, all the time. I began a YouTube channel with teaching videos and miracle testimonies, while praying for people in various places and locations. It has been a fabulous ministry, but like everything with the Lord, it was not to remain at that level. It was just a stepping stool to the most amazing teaching of this ministry, the crowning jewel, The Altar of Love.

The Altar of Love is my labor of love, one that has brought much joy and enlightenment, but only by the way of many trials and heartache. It is the culmination of 26 years of ministry through which were so many miracles, it would take several books to tell them all.

All-in-all, I never gave up on the Word, though at times, I could not see the hand of God in my situation. I decided long ago, I will trust my Father. Whether I understand the why or why not, ultimately, I will trust that my Father has my best interest at heart. My life is full of awesome testimonies, but how does one acquire a testimony unless he endures a test?

> *For I desire mercy and not sacrifice, And the knowledge of God more than burnt offerings.* Hosea 6:6

The New American Standard says it like this:

> *For I delight in loyalty rather than sacrifice, And in the knowledge of God rather than burnt offerings.*

But my favorite version of this verse is in the Living Bible:

> *I don't want your sacrifices, I want your love. I don't want your offerings, I want you to know me.*

The sheer volume of information, knowledge, and spiritual wisdom of the Father in this book will seem overwhelming. Please do not let it intimidate you. You can do this. You may need to reread parts of it a few times, but it will get in you. The wisdom of God will pour out on you and you will never be the same.

The Altar of Love will teach you how to overcome the works of darkness in your life and in the lives of the people you love. It is a process based upon the Word of God, that will break the cords of bondage that the enemy uses to keep people in perpetual sin. This sin is the barrier, which prevents them from receiving their healing and walking in spiritual victory. The Altar of Love will show you how to take the power away from the enemy and return it back to you... the one who was created to rule   from   the   beginning.

Table of Contents

Chapter One

The Altar of Love - Laying the Groundwork

My reawakening began A few years ago when I had a dream of being raptured. The dream began with me hovering about 500 feet in the air, when I noticed the coastline below. I specifically noticed the water and the different depths, thereof, when suddenly I began to shoot upward at hundreds of miles an hour. I recall being excited, thinking, This is it! This is the rapture. I am being raptured. Just a note to anyone that had held onto the doctrine that there is no rapture, I have but one thing to say, if there was no rapture, how did I get raptured? Certainly, God is not going to send us mixed signals, is He?

I cried out, "Father," and when I did, I stopped in mid air. My first thought was, "Oh no, why did I have to say anything?" Just then, in a loud thundering voice I heard, "Time as you know it is up. Every second, every minute, every hour, and every day, that I give you from this day forward, is by My grace alone. Prepare your heart to go home, it's time to go home." This dream changed my outlook on everything, because I now know that the age of grace is quickly coming to an end, any day now. The rapture is at hand and it is time to go and tell the people, but how to do that, I did not know. How would I say it? Who would believe a dream?

I took some time off from work, and after three days of prayer and fasting, I heard, *Get up... Go!* I jumped out of my chair, like I was going to run somewhere, but not knowing where to run, I said, "Go where? You told me to get my heart ready, so that's what I'm doing." He said, *Go and feed my*

sheep. I've been pouring into you for 25 years. Go and feed my sheep. Over the course of the next few days, He taught me how to move in the gift of healing and how to teach it to others. So, there I was, a man on a mission to tell people the time of the rapture is here and to be about my Father's business.

When I got saved, I was fortunate enough to have been trained in the Word by Jim Scalise. Jim is best described as a modern day Paul. He was a former drug dealer, whose clients were the who's-who of the 70's. Hollywood stars, sports athletes, rock legends, they all got their drugs from Jim. One day Jim opened his door to dozens of federal agents, guns drawn, pointed at his face. To hear him tell the story, there were so many guns in his face, there was no room for another pistol barrel. Jim received 17 life sentences and was destined to spend the remainder of his life behind bars.

As he lay on the cold concrete floor dying of pneumonia, feeling his very life slip away, he heard a guard walking by his cell. "Help me," he said, "Send me to the infirmary or I will die here." The guard responded, "You were man enough to get yourself in here, be man enough to get yourself well," and walked off. As he lay there sobbing, feeling his very life slip away, he opened his eyes and saw a Bible on his shelf that his mother had sent him. With all the energy he could muster, he got off the floor, grabbed the Bible off the shelf and not knowing where to start, fanned through it and opened to Mark 16:17, which seemed to come off the page at him in 3D. It read, *These signs will follow all who believe in my name, they will lay hands on the sick and they shall recover...*

His worldly upbringing, coupled with an almost delirious fever, left him unable to understand what he was reading or what it meant. As he pondered it, he thought, there are three things needed here: you have to believe in someone, you've got to have a hand, and there has to be a sick person. Then he thought, I don't know what to believe, but I have a hand and I'm sick, so I have two out of the three. So with that, he took his hand and laid it on his head and a warm feeling immediately came over his entire body as the power of Almighty God came upon him and healed him from head to toe. Not only did it take the sickness away, but it took all the evil, all the addiction, and every stronghold that held him in bondage.

From that day on, he vowed to dedicate his life to the Lord and he kept that vow. He began by going to church services, whenever they were held. After a few months, the prison minister unexpectedly missed the service and everyone sat there not knowing what to do. Once Jim realized the minister was not going to show, he went to the podium and began talking about the things he had learned. All the attendees, having known Jim, who he was and why he was there, laughed and mocked him. "You... you're going to minister to us? That's just great." Remember though, he had been cleansed of all the worldly lusts, desires and all the junk that goes with it. The embarrassment was gone, the offense was gone, the shame was gone, so none of what they said bothered him and he began to preach. Whenever he was asked how he got started in the ministry, he used to say, "I just showed up." He never missed a service and if the minister missed, then Jim preached more and more until he was leading the services regularly.

One day he received a call from his attorney. There was a problem with his case and he was to prepare for court the following day. To Jim's surprise, the judge threw out all 17 felony convictions and released him on a technicality. He became a full time prison minister, dedicating six days a week, and eight hours a day. Now a minister makes his living off the tithes and offerings of his church, but prisoners don't tithe. They don't have any money and if they did, they certainly would not be giving it away. So, how do you suppose he lived all those years? By pure faith alone! Try to imagine not knowing where your source of income would come from, but trusting the Lord to provide it. That was his life, and provide God did.

I personally remember being at his house one day as he told me how the Lord told him he was going to the Cayman Islands to lead some people to salvation and plant a new church. He said he was going in one week and when I asked if he had his tickets yet, he said he did not, nor did he have the money, and he had to buy them today so the money had to come on this day. The mailman had just pulled away from his box and Jim asked if I would go out and get his check. "Oh, did someone send you a check?" I replied. He responded, "Not that I know of, but if I'm going to go, one had better be there." I laughed to myself as I went to get the mail.

Now understand, my relationship with him was relatively new. He had prayed for me a time before and a miracle did transpire, but I was a relatively new believer and not really into the groove of all this Christianity stuff and I certainly did not fully understand the magnitude of this man's ministry. When I returned, he asked me what was there. I told him he had a few bills and a random letter. He asked me to open the letter and read it to him, so I did.

It read: *Dear Jim, You probably don't remember me, but I am one of the inmates you ministered to for months and months. I never really acknowledged you openly, but I listened every day as you stood in the hallway and preached to the cells. I never forgot what you preached and I never forgot you. I've been out for several years now. I have a successful business, a new wife and child, thanks to the Lord, and to you for being faithful. Recently, I felt the Lord telling me that I needed to bless you, so here is a check for $1,250. Be blessed my friend.*

Astonished, I looked up and said, "How much was your ticket? $1,240," he said, and from that day on I was hooked. I offered my services to him as often as I felt led, and gave him money for Bibles to give to the prisoners. He rarely asked for help, but whenever he did, I provided whatever he needed. I watched how he walked, how he acted, and how he reacted. He was the epitome of love. Never once did I see him get shaken or discouraged or anxious. He always walked in faith and love and miracles followed him everywhere he went. He was a modern day Paul, and I witnessed so many miracles that I could write a book on them alone.

Jim passed away in 2010 and I always felt like a part of me died with him. Today, I strive to live up to his model, to walk like him, in full faith and assurance that, if God said it, by gosh, He will do it. Jim's response to almost everything was, "Well, let's pray about it." His favorite teaching was Mark 4, the parable of the sower and for anyone familiar with me, it's my favorite, as well.

I tell the story about Jim to show that from my beginning in the ministry, I believed in miracles. They were not uncommon and after watching Jim perform hundreds, I just expected them. It was actually strange to us if we prayed for someone and didn't see a miracle. The times we didn't see miracles immediately manifest, they always presented themselves at a later date or in a different form. Miracles were commonplace with Jim. When the Lord began showing me about healing, He was teaching me deeper and more thoroughly than what I learned with Jim. I will explain this in detail as we go through The Altar of Love.

So, there I am, with all this new revelation of the soon coming rapture and marching orders from the Lord to feed His sheep and heal the sick. It is time to put it into practice. In my mind, I am thinking that church is the perfect place to test out this new gift God has given me. So, I'm hanging out in the lobby before the service, but something doesn't feel right, not here, not now, so instead of trying to force it, I just went in the service. After church, the same thing...no prompting, nothing, so I left and as I'm driving away, I am really confused. On the one hand, I want to try out this new tool, but on the other hand, I've got to be obedient. I thought, oh well, another time, I suppose.

I decided to go to the store to get some meat to make fajitas, and while I was shopping, I was talking to my brother on the phone. Unable to find the meat I was looking for, I turned to see this young female employee approaching me. I noticed that she was wearing a medical boot, limping and grimacing with every step. She said, "Can I help you?" Mind you, what I say next did not come from me. I did not rehearse it and please wait till the end before you judge it, because it makes sense in the end. I said, "Can I take your pain away?" My brother is on the other end of the phone listening to this play out. Puzzled by my response, she said, "What?" Again, I replied, "Let me take your pain away. How?" she asked. "Watch," I replied. Again, this is all surreal to me at the time, because I'm not really doing it, but the Holy Spirit inside me is. I took her by the hands and simply said, "I speak to the pain and I say, pain go." That's all I said.

We both just stood there for a few seconds and then I said, "Well, how does it feel?" She said, "Numb, it just feels numb." I asked, "On a scale of 1 to 10, what was your pain level at?" She said, "A 10." She said that she dropped a 200 lb piece of equipment on her foot and crushed all of her bones. I asked her what she did that hurt, so we could determine if she was healed or not. She said it hurt to simply walk, so I said, "Go walk around." She took about 10 steps away and came back and said it felt much better, but there was still a little pain left, yet nothing like before. So, I said, "Ok, let's do it again." She asked me how I did that, and I said, "I did it in the name of Jesus, I'll show you." This time I invoked the name of Jesus, and commanded the rest of the pain to go in Jesus' name and when I opened my eyes, she had tears pouring down her face. I asked her how it felt and she said it felt perfect. There was no pain at all. She asked me how she could repay me, which I found peculiar, but I told her all I wanted her to do was remember what we did and how we did it, so she could do it for someone else one day. I asked her if she was a believer and she said that she was. I told her that I was no more special than her and what I just did, she could do as well. She promised she would, gave me a huge hug, and walked away without a limp.

That was the first of many healing miracles God would do through me over the course of the next year, until He brought me The Altar of Love.

One day, in the mid 90's, I was sitting in my office when one of my black belt students asked to speak with me. Somehow, the conversation shifted to God. Knowing that he was raised by an atheist mother and an agnostic father, I ministered to him the best I knew how. I recall that I felt very good about how the conversation went. He was a long time student, probably 15 years at this point and we had a good relationship, and he respected me.

Upon his departure, I recall thinking to myself, That went well, good job. Then I heard the Holy Spirit say, very clearly, **Look up**, and when I did, I saw the Tae Kwon- Do encyclopedias and this is what I heard, *Just look at those encyclopedias, you know everything there is to know about Tae Kwon-Do, which has no value whatsoever when you expire, but how much do you really know about Me and my word?* I was floored. The word 'shamed' does not even begin to describe how disappointed I was in myself. He was right, I spent most of my life studying something that would be of no spiritual value to me, what-so-ever. It was time for me to rearrange my priorities.

Let me take a moment here to explain that Tae Kwon-Do, as I learned it from several Korean masters, had absolutely no occult background at all. There was no meditating, no chanting, no chi power, not one iota of anything that could or would attract demonic influence. I was trained by men with no interest in such things. It would best be compared to that of boxing or wrestling, with added kicks. It was like a sport to us, and we were jocks.

That said, I had begun to hunger for the Word of God and a close personal relationship with my Father and Jesus. As is my personality, I studied the Word the same way I trained in martial arts, like a maniac. I would read, study, and pray, each and every day for hours on end. The more I did, the more I learned, and the hungrier for wisdom I became. One day, after studying for hours, I was praying, and a loud audible voice came over me. Being relatively new at this, I wasn't hearing the subtle voice of the Holy Spirit yet, so when my Father wanted to talk to me, He always did it in a loud clear voice. This was one of those times, and I heard, I *did not give you the gifts and talents to teach so that you would teach Tae Kwon-Do. I used Tae Kwon-Do to teach you how to teach, so that you would teach my Word!*

I sat back on my heals, thinking about what the Lord just said to me when I heard my wife walking through the living room behind me. As I turned to her, she must have noticed something different with me, because she stopped and said, "What?" I said, "I think KID FIT is supposed to be a Christian Camp and I think I'm supposed to teach Bible study there." She said, matter of factly, "I've known that for about a year, just waiting for you to figure it out."

KID FIT was an after school and summer camp for kids that worked in conjunction, but as a separate entity of our Tae Kwon-Do program. The following day, we notified our customers that KID FIT would begin adding Bible study to the curriculum. The parents pushed back hard, and a day after that, only seven kids remained. Oddly enough, we were not shaken all that much. Our martial arts program was doing well enough, so we went forward with it. Within several months, word spread and we had grown right back to our original numbers.

Within 2 years, we had opened 2 other locations, and within 4 years, we had grown to 6 locations. By year 8, we had grown to 22 locations. We were preaching the Gospel throughout the entire city of Houston and these kids were getting saved and filled with the Holy Spirit. To this day, we have many former KID FIT kids that are preaching, teaching, and evangelizing all over the world.

Shortly after we converted our camp to a Christian camp, I was telling my father about a job offer I had received. A dear Christian friend of mine told me about a friend of his who had the largest window factory in the country and he needed a new president to run the company. He wanted someone who had experience and success running their own business, but the person had to be a devout Christian. My friend recommended me, and warned me that he would be calling with an offer very soon. He said the last president had just retired making half a million dollars a year and far more than we were making at the time.

Almost immediately after we hung up, I received a call from my earthly father. Now, you should probably know a little something about my dad. He was not a believer, not at this time, anyway. If you took all the knowledge of the Bible and threw it away, that is how much my father understood. He knew nothing and had absolutely no interest in it, whatsoever. He would not even allow me to talk about it to him. Whenever I did, his eyes would glaze over and he would just check out. With that, I proceeded to tell him about the job offer.

Mind you, my father was old school; the only talk I can ever recall him having with me was when I was 9. He came in my bedroom early in the morning, sat on the end of my bed, and woke me up. He patted my leg and said, "Son, the measure of a man is how much money he makes and how many women he sleeps with." Then he got up and walked out.

Yeah, you heard me, I was 9. You can imagine the kind of person I was until I got saved. Anyway, after I told him of this amazing offer, he paused for a few moments and said, "Didn't you just tell me that you had turned your program into a Christian program a few months ago and that it was beginning to do very well? Didn't you, also, say that the kids were getting saved and that they were performing miracles?" To say I was shocked would be an understatement. I was blown away.

This meant that he had to be listening to me when I was talking to him, so I responded, "Yes, it is doing well and the kids are getting saved daily." "Well," he said, "Sounds to me like this offer is from the Devil." I pulled the phone away from my ear and looked at it like it was diseased. What the heck did I just hear come out of my father's mouth? Are you kidding me? God could not have made a bigger impression on me than if a dog walked in on two feet and spoke those words himself. There is no way my father said that. His only concern was money and how much of it you made. This had to come from the Holy Spirit, and needless to say, I humbly declined the job offer. Fast forward to January 2015, I was beginning to sense a real urgency in my spirit. I started spending more time in the Word and praying in the spirit. I have this thing I do where I close my eyes, spin my Bible and flip it randomly, then I fan through it, so I have no clue if I'm coming from the back or the front. Wherever I land, that's what I would read that day. I don't do it all the time, just occasionally.

Well, one day I spun, flipped, and fanned through my Bible, and opened to Ezekiel 33. Feeling compelled to do so the next day, I opened again to Ezekiel 33. Thinking it was strange, but not seeing the big picture yet, I did it the next two days and lo and behold, Ezekiel 33. It wasn't until the fourth day that it dawned on me, and only after I began to ask why Ezekiel 33, did I realize, I'm a watchman. Good gracious, I'm a Watchman..."doh." It was a bit embarrassing that it took four days for me to figure it out.

Over the next year or so, I began following a few Christian channels on YouTube. One day, while considering my rapture dream, the fact that time is pretty well up, my calling to feed His sheep, the anointing to heal in the name of Jesus, and learning that I'm a watchman, I decided to begin my own YouTube channel. Which, in retrospect, I wish I had begun much sooner, but it is what it is. I enjoyed many of the channels that I followed, but I observed a void on YouTube. Paul described the spiritual immaturity of the Corinthians like this:

I have fed you with milk, and not with meat: for till now you were not able to bear it, neither yet now are you able. 1 Cor. 3:2

Nobody was teaching meat on YouTube. There were plenty of dreamers, and some Word related lessons, but nobody was teaching the deep things of God.

Since that was my first gifting, I decided to give YouTube a go. I am pleased with the outcome, although I fully expected it to grow much bigger, but not everyone is ready for meat. Most people want milk or soda. A soda message is sugary sweet to the taste and tickling to the ears, but of no value to anyone. It's the kind of message you might hear in a mega church, promising your best life now. The prosperity message is soda. My channel would be different from anything I had seen, as I would speak from my heart all the things that had been stored up all those years, as well as, all the new revelations I was receiving. I was going to be obedient and 'feed the sheep.'

By this time, the Lord was moving mightily, as many lives got touched, many more got healed, and many more got saved. I titled my YouTube channel by my actual name, Francis Santarose, because I decided that I didn't want to hide behind an alias. I would make myself accessible to whomever needed help. My goal was to teach all the marvelous lessons that my Father had taught me, as well as, recording random healings with my phone and uploading them on YouTube, as a testimony to the power of God in the name of Jesus.

One day, I was talking to one of my martial arts distributers, when I heard the Lord tell me the woman handling my account had pain in her back. I inquired, and she acknowledged it was true and she let me pray for her. Instantly, she was healed, and I got to minister to her. Four months and many miracle healings later, I get an email from her that said her back had begun hurting again, even worse than before. So I inquired of the Lord, and that was when He showed me The Altar of Love.

First, He said, as western medicine only treats the symptom, not the cause, likewise, I was only treating the symptom and not the actual cause or source of the sickness, pain or disease. That's when I saw The Altar of Love. The base and top was granite, but there were no legs. There was nothing written on the base, but I knew that it represented Jesus and Salvation. Just then, one leg came into my view and it moved in under one corner. Written on the leg was the word, Identity. Next, came the second leg with the word Authority, followed by the third leg which read, 'Power of Words.' So I'm looking at this Altar, with legs of Identity, Authority, and Power of Words, but the fourth leg is missing.

The Lord began ministering to my spirit and He said, *From now on, this is what I want you to teach and the order in which to teach it. First, get them to understand their Identity as My children. Next, teach them about a believer's Authority. Then tell them about the power of their words, but the last leg is the key.* He said, *You can understand your Identity, you can walk in Authority and power, you can even move mountains with your words, but without the last leg, the table will fall.* That's when I saw the fourth leg move into place and written on it was the word 'love.' I opened my laptop and proceeded to write everything that he told me and showed me.

Everyone on Earth is going to be judged and placed into one of two categories: sheep or goats, wheat or tears, believers or unbelievers. Sheep enter the Kingdom of Heaven and live for all eternity with the Father and Son, but the goats will be cast into outer darkness, where there is weeping and gnashing of teeth. Like a movie playing out before my eyes, I saw a story of the lives of some that loved God and obeyed His Word. This love, devotion, and obedience would lead them to an eternity with God.

As awe-inspiring as this was, I also saw the story of the rebellious at heart... those that had outright rejected God, as well as, those that once served Him, but had gone back to the world. He, also, showed me those that had fallen for the false grace, once saved always saved doctrine. Satan has deceived them into thinking that because they said a prayer 18 years earlier, they could live any way they want, and walk in willful sin, because they thought they were saved by grace. They have no remorse for their horrendous behavior. They don't feel the need to repent or ask forgiveness, because they are covered by grace. All the while, they ignore the dozens and dozens of Bible verses that say otherwise, thereby, playing Russian Roulette with their salvation. For these goats, someday, with deep anguish, will regret for eternity. It is a deception and a doctrine of demons.

You see, man is a rebellious and wicked creature. We have rebelled against the living God. We have cursed Him, challenged Him, denied Him and even worshiped His worst enemy. It's not our fault. We were born this way. It is our nature. Yet, even after all that, He never stopped loving us. He never gave up on us, because His love is not dependent upon us. There are no preconceived requirements to get it. His love is unconditional. It never ends and it never fails. We have until the day we die to find this love, and all throughout the Bible we are instructed to go after this love, to seek it out, as one seeks a treasure.

What would you do if you learned of a treasure buried right in your own back yard? You'd get a shovel and dig, nonstop, until you found your treasure. This is the underlying theme of the gospel of Jesus Christ. Jesus is that treasure... *For if any man finds Him and makes Him Lord, He shall have eternal life. But woe to him who says in his heart, "I am young; let me eat, drink and be merry, for there is plenty of time in my latter years for God."*

Death is an enigma, and for anyone without the Lord Jesus, eternity is a long, long time. For death knows no boundaries, sees no color, cares not for your title, honors no fame, and is no respecter of age. It comes when it wants, shows up where it wants, and takes whomever it wants.

Beginning in the book of Genesis, after God created the earth, He creates his crowning jewel, man. God blesses Adam and Eve and gives them dominion over His creation. Adam did not own the earth, but he was given the lease to it, the legal right to rule it.

God blessed them and said to them, *Be fruitful and multiply, and fill the earth, and subdue it; and rule over the fish of the sea and over the birds of the sky and over every living thing that moves on the earth.* Then God said, *Behold, I have given you every plant yielding seed that is on the surface of all the earth, to every beast of the earth and to every bird of the sky and to every living thing that moves on the earth which has life, I have given every green plant for food; and it was so.* Gen. 1:28-30

This thing called dominion is not only a great honor, but it yields great power. With that great power, however, comes an even greater responsibility. Along with dominion, Adam and Eve were given the legal right to rule and rein as king and queen on planet Earth. It, and everything in it, was subject to them and their offspring. Jesus refers to dominion on multiple occasions, but He uses a different word to describe it. He calls it Authority.

Chapter Two

The Antagonist

Before his eviction from Heaven, Satan was known as Lucifer. Isaiah 14:12 says, *How art thou fallen from Heaven, O Lucifer, son of the morning star! You said in your heart, I will ascend into Heaven. I will exalt my throne above the stars of God. I will sit on the mountain of the assembly, in the far north. I will ascend above the heights of the clouds; I will be like the most High...* You can almost feel the arrogance of Satan, but God responds, *But you will be brought down to Hell into the deepest regions of the Pit.*

In Ezekiel 28, God goes into even more detail regarding the fall of Satan, as well as, what He was like before the fall. *Because your heart is lifted up, And you say, am a God, I sit in the seat of God's, In the midst of the seas, Yet you are a man, and not a God, Though you set your heart as the heart of a God, Behold, you are wiser than Daniel! There is no secret that can be hidden from you! With your wisdom and your understanding, You have gained riches for yourself, And gathered gold and silver into your treasuries; By your great wisdom in trade you have increased your riches, And your heart is lifted up, because of your riches.*

Therefore thus says the Lord GOD: Because you have set your heart as the heart of a God, Behold, therefore, I will bring strangers against you, The most terrible of the nations; And they shall draw their swords against the beauty of your wisdom, And defile your splendor. They shall throw you down into the Pit, And you shall die the death of the slain In the midst of the seas... Ezekiel 28:6-8

Adding insult to injury, Satan, was thrown out of Heaven in front of all his followers, the fallen ones. This account is recorded in even more detail in Ezekiel 28:12-19: *You were the seal of perfection, Full of wisdom and perfect in beauty. You were in Eden, the garden of God; Every precious stone was your covering: The sardius, topaz, and diamond, Beryl, onyx, and jasper, Sapphire, turquoise, and emerald with gold. The workmanship of your timbrels and pipes Was prepared for you on the day you were created. You were the anointed cherub who covers; I established you; You were on the holy mountain of God; You walked back and forth in the midst of fiery stones. You were perfect in your ways from the day you were created, until iniquity was found in you. By the abundance of your trading You became filled with violence within, And you sinned; Therefore I cast you as a profane thing, Out of the mountain of God; And I destroyed you, O covering cherub, From the midst of the fiery stones. Your heart was lifted up because of your beauty; You corrupted your wisdom for the sake of your splendor; I cast you to the ground, I laid you before kings, That they might gaze at you. You defiled your sanctuaries By the multitude of your iniquities, By the iniquity of your trading; Therefore I brought fire from your midst; It devoured you, And I turned you to ashes upon the earth In the sight of all who saw you. All who knew you among the peoples are astonished at you; You have become a horror, And shall be no more forever.*

It appears like the problem is solved when Satan is expelled from the mountain of God, but let this serve as a lesson to everyone, this enemy of ours is very cunning and He's **never** out of the game. As soon as, Satan heard about this thing called dominion, the Authority that Adam had been given. He becomes outraged with jealousy. Considering the narcissist that He is, Satan must be thinking, That's my Authority, that's my dominion. How dare God take what was rightfully mine and give it to... a mere mortal. Having been stripped of all His spiritual powers upon His expulsion from the Kingdom of Heaven, Satan devises a plan to steal Authority away from Adam.

Now I don't like to give the Devil accolades for anything, but this was a brilliant plan and He puts it into motion flawlessly. You see, Satan is a master liar, and Jesus himself called Satan the father of all lies. So good at lying was He, that He, actually, convinced one third of the angels in Heaven to rebel with Him. These angels had a personal relationship with the Father, they served Him daily, they walked among His creation, upon streets paved with gold, and they basked in His abounding love. If Satan could deceive God's personal servants, how much easier would it be to deceive a human?

Before the fall, Satan had the most exalted position, full of wisdom and perfection. After the fall, Satan had nothing. No kingdom, no power, and no Authority. He was lower than a human, and it fueled a fire of hatred, jealousy and rage towards mankind.

Adam, on the other hand, had been made in the image of the almighty God. He had the actual spirit of the living God inside him and he was given a kingdom on Earth to rule. Like the snake He is, Satan determines that Eve is the weak link and plays her like a fiddle. Eve is naive and gullible, and Satan, being such an accomplished liar, and the most beautiful of all of God's creations, seduces her to sin. With just a few words

Satan can make you begin to doubt everything you know to be true. He can take that self doubt and turn it into extreme sadness. With a bit more coaxing, He can turn sadness into full blown depression. With depression, just the right circumstance, and a bit more nudging, He can talk you into self-mutilation and even suicide. And He can pull off that scam in a matter of weeks with some people.

But why? Why does He hate us so much? Because He's jealous of us and He hates God. He knows that there's nothing He can do to hurt God, because God is too powerful for Him. He, also, knows God well enough to know how much love is in His heart towards His creation. He knows that if God took so much care in actually forming us with His own hands, that we must be very special to Him. He knows that God is holy and sin has no place in His kingdom, so his plan is two-fold. First, by deceiving man to sin, the Devil would create a barrier between God and His children. This would establish eternal separation from God, whereby, the Devil can take sinful man to Hell and torture him forever.

You see, loneliness exists, because Satan is lonely, depression exists, because Satan is depressed, hatred exists, because Satan is full of hate. Every bitter, spiteful, mean, unforgiving hurtful emotion comes from the Devil, and He projects them on us, because misery loves company. Satan wants us to be just like him. When God's sees us in our unredeemed state, we look, think and act more like Satan, than we do our own Father. Jesus said, *Broad and wide is the road to Hell and many go that way, but narrow and small is the way to Heaven, and only a few go there.* Why? Because we're gullible, we believe the lie and drink the cool aid.

Satan's second goal was to steal the dominion, the legal right, the Authority, that was intended for us, God's children. Satan put His plan in motion and, voila, it worked perfectly. Adam and Eve handed over their dominion and they never even put up a fight.

For the next 4,000 years, Satan ruthlessly wielded this power called Authority and cast man into a prison of horror with no chance of escape, no hope at all. In Satan's prison, man is abused, starved, beaten, raped, tortured, and even murdered. So horrible are the conditions of this prison, that over time, man begins to forget who they were created to be, what they were created to be... children of living God. As generations pass, man begins to look more and more like their captors, and less like their Father. Eventually, they've taken on every characteristic and quality of the demons that enslaved them and no longer resemble their Father, at all. The Father's heart is breaking for His children, that now look more like His mortal enemy, than Him.

Mans predicament is bleak. It appears like an impossible situation. There they are, in a prison, with no chance of parole or escape, and worse yet, headed for an eternity of torture and Hellfire, because this enemy only comes to kill, steal and destroy. Furthermore, man is without excuse. Rebellion against God has given Satan the Authority to do this to them. There they are, in prison, crying out for help, but no one can hear them. There's no escaping this prison. It's a fortress of solid steel surrounded by 16 foot demon guards who take pleasure in torture and pain. Woe to mankind. Only horror awaits him. Any moments of pleasure and joy are only a brief and temporary feeling. They are a mask, a deception that hides from man the real Hell that awaits him. As horrible and hideous the conditions of the prison are, it pales in comparison to the pit of fire that awaits man, because this enemy is coming to kill him and take him to that pit for all eternity.

This enemy, the Devil, can't be reasoned with, he can't be bargained with, he knows no remorse, he doesn't take vacations, never gets sick and he absolutely, positively will not stop until we are dead and burning with Him in Hell. And let's not forget, he has the Authority, the legal right to do so, because of all the unrepentant sin we have engaged in.

The Great King & The Wicked King

There was a great and powerful king who had found evil in the heart of his number one general. Upon being banished from the kingdom of the Great King, this general set up his own kingdom, calling himself a king. This evil wicked king had deceived many of the Great King's officers, that were under his command. They joined the evil king and helped him set up his wicked kingdom. One day, the wicked king raided a village, that belonged to the Great King and stole all his children, about 70 in number.

The wicked king threw them in dungeons and began to torture them unmercifully. They were beaten daily, tortured, and abused physically, emotionally, and sexually. Their captors threw their food at them, so they were forced to eat it off the floor like animals. Days turned into weeks, weeks turned into months, and months turned into years, until the children of the Great King began to forget their kingly heritage. Years turned into decades, and soon new generations were born into this slavery, so that they knew nothing of their royal lineage. Other than some vague stories about the Great King, who would come and save them one day, they had lost all hope and memory of who they really were.

One day the Great King instructed his first born son to go and retrieve his children. In a surprise assault, the son breaks into the prison and opens the gates for all to escape, only to find, few seemed willing to go. Most had grown so accustomed in their environment that they didn't want to leave. It was their home, they were comfortable there. He begged and pleaded with them to go, but only a few believed he was who he said he was. The rest mocked and insulted him until he finally left with the few who would believe. Upon arriving at the Great Kings palace, they were ushered into a dining hall where they were instructed to sit and eat with their Father the King. Hung over their chair was the same robe worn by the King and the son. A gold ring was sitting in the center of their placemat, and they were instructed to put on the ring and robe to symbolize their restoration of Sonship to the King.

It was all so overwhelming to them and the reaction was varied. Some put on the ring and robe and snuggled into their seats and received the delicacies that were placed before them. Others removed the rings, threw off the robes, and tossed their plates to the floor, eating off the ground, just as they did in prison. They were unable to fully receive the love and generosity of their Father the King. The Father and Son wept for the children who wanted to return to their former prison. Within time, the children who stayed began to understand who they were as children and heirs to the throne. They began to walk confidently and behaved as children of the King, rather than slaves. They grew grateful to the King for making a way of escape and thankful for the son who risked his life to save them.

This story illustrates our predicament today. Most Christians have no concept of who they are, something we will cover in great detail in the next chapter. Our identity is just one of the things our enemy has masterfully hidden from us. The Catholic Church, working as an agent of the Devil used to kill people for reading a Bible. Why? Because Satan knows if the Word goes in you, the Word will come out of you. Jesus said, ***Nothing comes out of a man except for what is in his heart.*** Therefore, the Catholic Church was, and still is, an agent of the Devil to prevent masses of people from reading their Bibles to develop a personal relationship with the God of creation.

Don't get me wrong here, I'm not calling out Catholics without cause. I was born and raised a Catholic. I am intimately aware of their deception and depravity. Many Catholic priests are pedophiles, who, upon detection, are simply ushered to a new parish to continue molesting children. Catholicism, the largest so-called, "Christian church," in the world, is nothing more than a giant serpent, a creation of Satan himself, designed to provide a semblance of religion, all the while leading billions away from Jesus, and to the Pope.

Pope Francis, among many blasphemous statements, just recently said that having a personal relationship with Jesus was dangerous. He claimed that going to your priest was a better way to hear from God. But that's not even really that remarkable a statement, because anyone with a lick of sense knows the Pope is an agent of the Devil. No, the real snake presented itself recently when Kenneth Copeland, widely known as the head of the modern charismatic Christian movement, the captain of the once saved-always saved (OSAS) doctrine, proclaimed publicly that the Pope was the man to follow. Kenneth considered the Pope his new hero. Look, I could write an entire book about the Catholic Church, but not at this time. Suffice it to say, the Catholic Church is a big giant snake.

Following Satan's temptation of Jesus in the desert, the Bible says that Satan left the Lord, but only for a season. I have learned over the years that the Devil would be back many times in different ways and in different forms and it was up to me, through a close personal relationship with my Father by virtue of what Jesus did on the cross, to recognize the attack and stand courageously when the attack comes.

In Ephesians chapter 6, Paul describes the Armor of God. *Finally my brethren, be strong in the Lord and the power of his might. Put on the whole armor of God that you may be able to stand against the wiles of the Devil. For we do not wrestle against flesh and blood, but against principalities, against powers, against the rulers of the darkness of this age, and against spiritual hosts of wickedness in the Heavenly places. Therefore, take up the whole armor of God, that you may be able to withstand in the evil day, and having done all, to stand.*

Paul uses these two words, stand and withstand very specifically. Withstand *anthistemi;* means to stand against. The verb suggests vigorously opposing, bravely resisting, standing face-to-face against an adversary. While imprisoned in Rome, Paul wrote Ephesians. Confined and awaiting trial, Paul sees the church as the body of Christ and God's tool to overthrow the powers of darkness. With a Roman soldier standing in front of him, Paul writes this section using everyday things in the natural, to describe the supernatural. To stand or withstand is really a two-part word, which implies preparing for the day of battle, but more importantly, standing courageously, when that day arrives.

Take war for example; we obviously would never send kindergarteners into battle. Instead, we take young men and women in the prime of their life, and train them to run, jump, climb, dig, fight, shoot, drive tanks, fly planes, and captain ships. After much training, we send them to battle. What good would it be, however, if when in the heat of battle, they turned and ran away in fear?

Through the words **stand** and **withstand**, Paul is encouraging us to pray, fellowship and study the scriptures, so that we may be able to **stand** on the day evil arrives. Like a good soldier, trained in the art of war, we are to take the knowledge we have obtained from our study and apply it by confessing the Word. But even more importantly, we must **stand** courageously in faith, until victory has been achieved.

The evil day is the day your child contacts a fever of 105, the day the company lays you off after 25 years of dedicated service, the day the doctor says you have terminal cancer, or the day your best friend lay in critical care after a tragic car accident.

The completion of standing comes when we take Authority over sickness and command that fever to leave in the name of Jesus, stand firmly upon the promises of God to restore sevenfold what the Devil has stolen, believe that by the stripes of Jesus we were healed, and bind the spirit of cancer and command it to bow to the name that's above every name, Jesus.

The next part of Ephesians 6 is just as powerful as the first part. *Stand therefore, having girded your waist with truth, having put on the breastplate of righteousness and having shod your feet with the preparation of the gospel of peace; above all, taking the shield of faith with which you will be able to quench all the fiery darts of the wicked one. And take the helmet of salvation, and the sword of the Spirit, which is the word of God; praying always with all prayer and supplication in the Spirit, being watchful to this end with all perseverance and supplication for all the saints and for me, that utterance may be given to me, that I may open my mouth boldly to make known the mystery of the gospel, for which I am an ambassador in chains; that in it I may speak boldly, as I ought to speak.*

Let me make one thing perfectly clear, the armor of God is not a prayer that you pray over yourself each day before you leave the house. Well, let me rephrase that. You can, but it doesn't do any good. The armor of God is a lifestyle you live, not a prayer you pray. For example, Paul says to take up the helmet of salvation. Does that mean you have to pray to be saved every day? No, I am saved through my faith in Jesus, not because I pray for the armor of God.

Let's begin with, 'having girded your waist with truth.' Jesus is the truth. He said, *I am the way the truth and the life.* Jesus is the Word. John 1:1 says, *In the beginning was the Word and the word was with God and the Word was God. He was with God in the beginning.* Jesus is the Word, the Word is the Truth, and therefore, Jesus is the truth. As it is written, *Let God be true and every man a liar.* Everything that opposes the Word is a lie, so we are instructed to gird our waist with Jesus, the truth. But what does it mean to gird your waist? In the first century, they did not have underwear, people went commando, that is, they were foot loose and fancy free down there. However, being free flowing down there is not the best thing for a man in battle. While engaging in athletics, as well as, physical confrontations like war, men used their tunics like a giant diaper to make everything nice and snug down there. It was called, 'girding your waist,' which implied, getting ready for battle. Therefore, girding your waist with truth means to get ready for battle with Jesus by your side. It implies sowing the Word of God in the midst of your battle.

Next, Paul says, *Having put on the breastplate of righteousness.* A breastplate covers your chest, which houses your heart, so the breastplate protects the heart. A blow to the heart would certainly kill a soldier, so putting on the breastplate of righteousness symbolizes saving your spiritual life from Hell. We are the righteousness of God in Christ Jesus. Hebrews 10:26 says, *If we sin willingly after we receive the knowledge of the truth, there no longer remains a sacrifice for sins.* When Paul says we, he's including himself in the mix, he's talking to Christians. Willful sin is akin to taking off your breastplate of righteousness, which exposes you to possible spiritual death. We are expected to walk in righteousness, but if we sin, which really just means to miss the mark, we are to repent. 1 John 1:9 says, *If we confess our sins, He is faithful and just to forgive us and cleans us from all unrighteousness.*

The next piece of armor is footwear. *And having shod your feet with the preparation of the gospel of peace.* This, obviously, implies to prepare for the day of battle by reading your Word.

Remember, the ultimate victory comes from quoting the Word of God like Jesus in the desert, but it's pretty difficult to quote a Word that you do not know. The only way to quote the Word is if you've been reading and memorizing it for years. A soldier would not perform well on a first century battlefield without shoes, and we're not going to fare well in battle if we cannot quote the Word.

Regarding the next piece of armor, Paul writes... *above all, taking the shield of faith.* Above all does not imply that it is of greater value, just that it is in addition to the others. *Above all, taking the shield of faith with which you will be able to quench all the fiery darts of the wicked one.* The fiery darts of the wicked one are trials, tribulations, and circumstances brought on and made worse or exacerbated by the enemy. To quench the fiery darts is to extinguish, to put a stop to or cause to cease and desist the plots, plans, lies, traps, and snares of the Devil. Ponder this question, is Paul telling us to petition the Father to defend us from these fiery darts, or expecting us to do it ourselves? This question will be answered in great detail in the chapter titled Authority.

The Bible says, *Without faith, it is impossible to please God.* Faith is paramount here. If you want to be able to stand against the wiles of the Devil and quench his fiery darts, you must believe that you can. That is why it is called the shield of faith. The word 'shield' in this verse, comes from the Greek word thyreós, Strong's Concordance #2375. It is a full-body shield and refers to God's in-working of faith, i.e.: **the shield of faith** protects the whole believer, by covering the whole person in spiritual warfare.

The second to last piece of armor is the most important of all, the Helmet of Salvation. The helmet protects the soldier from a blow to the head, which would surely be a death blow. This symbolizes protection from spiritual death and eternal separation from God.

The last in the list of the armor of God is not a piece of armor at all. It is the only offensive weapon God has given us, The Sword of the Spirit, which is The Word of God. I will cover the awesome power of the Word of God in Chapter 6, The Power of the Word of God. It is worth noting that of all the pieces of the Armor of God, much like a hospital gown, none are designed to cover your back. This is because we are never expected to run like a coward. You must be willing to stand your ground and fight.

There has been an epic battle between man and Satan since the days of Adam. It was a one sided battle for four thousand years, because Satan had the most powerful weapon in the world at his disposal, the Authority that Adam handed him. Satan is spiritual, while we are physical. Because of that, He knows it is nearly impossible for us to wrap our minds around the fact that we are not necessarily fighting the things we can see, but the real fight is with the things we cannot see. 2 Corinthians 4:18 says, *So we fix our eyes not on what is seen, but on what is unseen. For what is seen is temporary, but what is unseen is eternal.* Paul is making a very clear distinction between the spiritual realm and the natural realm and, in doing so, he's instructing us to focus our attention on the root of the problem, not the symptoms. Jesus used parables to help people understand spiritual concepts, when placed within a natural context.

Suppose you were visiting a friend in a foreign country, and you had never heard of bullfighting before and he said that he wanted to take you to see a bullfight. At the stadium, you see a tiny man, 5'5," 125 lbs, wearing pink satin. He's skinny as a twig, and looking extremely effeminate in his pink wardrobe. From the other end, hidden behind a large wooden gate is something that appears to be big, fierce, and angry and the handlers can barely keep it contained within the gate. When released, you are amazed by the sheer size of the beast. He is 1,500 lbs of pure muscle with two very sharp horns; a most imposing creature and you're thinking, this is not going to be a fair fight.

As the two approach each other in the center of the field, the bull snorts, growls, kicks up some dirt, and readies for his death blow. The bullfighter, calmly pulls out his red cape, and when he does, the bull takes his eyes off of the bullfighter and puts them on the cape. Now, that bullfighter is no fool. He's been doing this for years and he keeps his distance from the cape, carefully observing the habit of the bull, as he takes his first pass. Some bulls hook left, some hook right. This particular bull hooks up and to the left, therefore, the champion bullfighter switches sides, so the bull is hooking away from him. Upon each pass, the bullfighter hits the bull in the neck with a pointed dart designed to breakdown the tendons in the neck of the bull. Exhausted from running, and barely able to hold his head up any longer from the darts, the bullfighter goes in for the kill.

This is a perfect portrayal of the battle between us and Satan. We are the bull with all the power and Authority in the name of Jesus, and Satan is the wimpy little bullfighter that has been stripped of his spiritual powers. There really should be no contest, but Satan is a champion bullfighter with thousands of years of experience at killing, steeling, and destroying. And while He has been stripped of his spiritual powers, He brilliantly uses the only tool at His disposal, and that tool is deception. His strategic use of the cape is designed to take our attention away from Him and put it on our situation, our spouse, our kids, our job, whatever He can use to redirect our focus.

Another scripture that accurately describes how the enemy works is found in 1 Peter, but there is more to this verse than meets the eye.

Be sober, be vigilant because your adversary, the Devil, walks about like a roaring lion seeking whom he may devour. 1 Peter 5:8

On the surface, you can clearly see the meaning, but there is a reason Peter uses a lion to illustrate his point. On the surface, to be sober is to be temperate, clear-headed, restrained and aware, while the opposite of sober is drunk. Drunk people are dim-witted, foolish and stupid. Because their senses are dulled from the alcohol they are slow to react, if they react at all. Drunk people are often completely unaware of their surroundings.

To be sober is to be alert, be aware, and to be on guard. To be vigilant is to be ready to take action at a moment's notice and with a diligent heart. Together they indicate that we should be ever ready to respond to an attack from an enemy that has no shame, knows no remorse, does not sleeps, and takes no vacations.

The hidden wisdom of this verse was never intended to be hidden at all, but this is where time and geographical differences prevent us from understanding the real meaning. Lions are territorial beasts, and they will stay in the area they have established as their own, even if the food source dries up with the rain. The African plains have rainy seasons and dry seasons. During the rainy seasons, the food supply is plentiful with gazelle, wildebeests, water buffalo, and more, so the lion has his fill. However, when the rainy season ends, the animals migrate to other regions, but the lion stays to guard his territory.

At the height of the drought, the lion is near starvation and must resort to feeding on rodents that burrow underground. As the lion walks about, he roars loudly and slams his big paw on the ground next to the rodent holes. If the rodent was smart, they would just hang tight and do nothing, because as long as they are in their hole, they are safe. However, the roaring of the lion and the slamming of his paw causes the rodent to panic and flee his hole, where the lion waits to pounce. Once again, the Devil, like the lion, uses the only thing he's got... deception. And we, like the rodent, fall for it every time.

There have been demonic forces following you around your entire life, whispering lies, and encouraging you to cheat, steal, rebel, fornicate, use drugs and alcohol, cause strife, murmur, and complain, etc. If it is sin, the Devil is behind it somewhere, and all the while he is recording your response. He takes note of the way you respond physically and emotionally to every given situation. Did traffic cause you to lose your temper? Did that name you were called hurt your feelings? How did you react when the spirit of depression or suicide planted their thoughts like a farmer plants a seed? Did you entertain the ideas by thinking about them, or worse yet, did you discuss them with anyone?

Can Satan get you to talk to yourself, out loud, by repeating the lies He's whispering in your ear? If so, you might as well sign your death warrant now, because that is all He needs to gain legal entrance to kill, steal, and destroy you, or someone you love. The only time you should be talking to yourself is when you are confessing the Word of God over yourself or someone you are standing for in faith. If God says it about you, that's what you say. Anything else is a lie from the pit of Hell, and it shouldn't come out of your mouth.

With the exception of Demonic possession, which we will delve into later, the Devil cannot make you do anything; He can only suggest it and encourage us to do it. That is why 1 Peter 5:8 says, **Be sober, be vigilant,** in regards to his schemes. Being sober, being vigilant is the only way we will be able to follow Paul's advice about examining our thought life. Your thought life is the Alternate life you live through the thoughts and intents of your heart and mind. Everyone has a thought life and it doesn't always reflect the way people appear on the outside. Hypocrites, liars, cheaters, thieves, adulterers and the like have a thought life that usually opposes their outward appearance. A polluted thought life will eventually lead to worldly, lustful behavior.

For people without Jesus, there is no moral compass, no higher standard compelling them to behave. The only way to tell if an unbeliever is a person of integrity, is over time. Being a believer is no guarantee that one will behave righteously in any given situation, however, the Word of God is a constant reminder of proper conduct and they will receive promptings from the Holy Spirit when they are behaving improperly.

> *...bringing every thought into captivity to the obedience of Christ.* 2 Corinthians 10:5

Try this, when a thought comes, test it by asking yourself a question: Is this from God or the Devil? You may ask, How will I know who it is from? Unless you are completely devoid of common sense, or lack any social skills, whatsoever, the answer to the question is always self-explanatory, even to a fool.

For instance, you are late for an important job interview, because of unexpected traffic. Realizing your tardiness, begins to cause anxiety and fear. Maybe your spouse caused you to be late and anger is, also, present. A sober, vigilant believer quickly notices the onset of those negative emotions and recognizes they are not from God and immediately begins to pray about the situation. "Heavenly Father I praise your holiness. You are mighty in battle and compassionate towards your children. You are great and your mercy endures forever. Your Word says to be anxious for nothing, but in all things through prayer, supplication with thanksgiving to make our requests known to You. And Your peace, which surpasses all understanding, will guard my heart and mind in Christ Jesus. Therefore, I turn this situation over to you. I refuse to worry any longer.

Revelations 3:8 says, *I have set before you an open door, and no one can shut it.* If that job is for me, nothing can stop it. In the name of Jesus, manage the traffic on my behalf and minister to the hearts and minds of the person giving the interview today. Your Word says what was intended for evil, God can use for good, and I trust, Father, that you are able to do exceedingly and abundantly, beyond anything I am able to think or even imagine, and I have a pretty good imagination. If this interview, however, is not profitable for me, I will assume that you have a better job lined up. One with better hours, better pay, closer to home, and in a more favorable work environment. Now, I thank you for doing it in Jesus name, Amen."

Every trial that you go through is just an opportunity for your Father to show his endless love, compassion, mercy and power towards you or through you to bless someone else. One of the most powerful tools you have to lead your friends and loved ones to the saving grace of Jesus Christ is a powerful testimony.

And they overcame him by the blood of the Lamb and the word of their testimony. Revelations 12:11

You will never have a testimony, however, unless you go through a test.

In this world you will have tribulation; but be of good cheer, I have overcome the world. John 16:33

Chapter Three

Identity: Leg 1 of The Altar of Love

Who are You Anyway?

The story of the Great King and the Evil King accurately illustrates the first leg of The Altar of Love, Identity. Most of the children had forgotten who they were and were unable to receive the benefits of their Father. In Psalm 103, David discusses the benefits of God that are available to His children.

> *Bless the LORD, O my soul;*
>
> *And all that is within me, bless His holy name!*
>
> *Bless the LORD, O my soul, And forget not all His benefits:*
>
> *Who forgives all your iniquities,*
>
> *Who heals all your diseases,*
>
> *Who redeems your life from destruction,*
>
> *Who crowns you with loving kindness and tender mercies,*
>
> *Who satisfies your mouth with good things,*
>
> *So that your youth is renewed like the eagle's.* Psalm 103

David instructs us not to forget our benefits, but very often they are forgotten. One day, I answered the door to a Kirby vacuum salesman. Because I had a martial arts facility that needed to be vacuumed daily, it seemed like we were buying a new vacuum every few months. At $150 a pop, I determined it would be a good investment to get a Kirby, which is considered the best made vacuum in the world, and I expected it to last a lifetime. $1,400 later, my wife, upon arrival and seeing the new Kirby vacuum, said she'd never leave me home alone again.

A few months later our business was broken into and all my computers, monitors, printers, and even my Kirby was stolen. Who steals a vacuum? Hello! The loss of my computers was devastating, especially considering they held the newly completed manuals to both the KID FIT Christian Camp, as well as, the Martial Arts program. I had spent the last five years writing the manuals, so we could begin franchising, and everything was gone. As devastated as that was, and it was, I could not get over the fact that they stole my new Kirby. While complaining about it one day, Angela chastised me, saying, "You've lost everything, all the computers, all the data, all the manuals and the only thing you are concerned about is that stupid vacuum." If it wasn't so funny, it would have been embarrassing. Months later, I opened my American Express bill to find an ad for their theft protection program, saying, all lost or stolen items purchased with your American Express will be replaced in full. Immediately, I called American Express and spoke to a rep. She confirmed the program was available for me, but when I faxed her my police report she noticed that my case had passed the statute of limitations which was set at six months. She said, had you known your benefits, you would have been fully reimbursed.

As I hung up the phone, I heard the Holy Spirit say, Psalm 103. I quickly opened my Bible and read it. As I sat pondering, I heard clear as day, if you had known your benefits, you would have recovered all, likewise, if you know and do not forget My benefits you will always be made whole. I read them again, but this time I read it with a different mindset, one that I would use every time I read my Bible. I read it like every Word was a promise from my Father directly to me... a Father who is incapable of lying, so it has to be true. Now, read it again with that mindset:

Who forgives all your iniquities, Who heals all your diseases,

> *Who redeems your life from destruction, Who crowns you with loving kindness and tender mercies, Who satisfies your mouth with good things, so that your youth is renewed like the eagle's.* Psalm 103:4

The modern day church has no understanding of who they are as Children of God. Oh, I know that we say we do, and we sing songs that say, "I'm a child of God," but we really have no clue and it shows by our behavior. Granted, Satan has done a good job hiding our Identity from us, because He knows that if we actually get the understanding of who we are, He's all but done for.

Recalling my vision of the legs moving in under The Altar of Love, I wondered if the order of the legs was significant and I was told that, in fact, they were. Identity was first, because without an understanding of who you are, there is no way to receive all the blessings and benefits our Father has in store for us. It all begins with a proper understanding of our Identity. When I began teaching The Altar of Love, I did it as though it were a case I was taking on and the very first question I would ask is, "Who are you?" Depending upon their response, I knew how and where to begin. Most people would begin by telling me about themselves and their history or how they got into the predicament they are in. I had to get them to understand that their identity is not a result of their circumstances, their upbringing, their successes, or their failures. It's not their heritage, their skin color, their politics, or their beliefs. Our identity must be rooted and grounded in one simple fact, that we are children of the most high God and anything else is foolishness.

Of the many cases that I have done, there was one reoccurring theme... it seemed as though I was their last resort. They had tried everything. Some had spent hundreds of thousands of dollars on doctors and surgery. Others had gone to demonologists and paid them large amounts of money, but none of it helped any of them. Now, don't get me wrong, I'm not taking credit for anything other than being obedient and doing what the Father tells me to do. I didn't know any of this until the Father showed me that day, and everything that I do is done in the name of Jesus. I am humbled by all of this and I constantly ask God, Why me? Why not some notable preacher in a mega church? I've have not yet received an answer.

I begin every case with John 1:12, *But to all who did receive him, who believed in his name, he gave the right to become Children of God.* Notice that it says, "To all who did receive Him." It says that, because those that do not receive Jesus as Lord, are not Children of God. While promoting his One World Religion, by trying to unite Christians, Jews and Muslims, the Pope foolishly claimed that we are all Children of God, but what did Jesus say? Jesus called the Pharisees Children of the Devil. That's a far cry from a Child of God. The Word is clear here, *But to all who did receive Him, who believed in His name, He gave the right to become Children of God.*

There is a big difference between a right and a privilege. A privilege is something you earn, but a right is granted to you by law. When we receive Jesus as our Lord and believe on His name, we are granted the right to become Children of God, by law. We do not have to earn the status of being a Child of God. It is a right. Contrary to popular belief, not everyone is a Child of God. Only those who have made Jesus Lord of their lives and believe in the power in His name, possess this right.

Do not be misled. The basis of this right is two-part. ***But to all who did receive Him, who believed in His name...*** There are plenty of people who say a sinners prayer, receiving Him as Lord, but you'd never know it by observing their life, because there is no belief or faith in His name or in the power of His name and His Word. Their basis for salvation loosely hangs solely upon a one-time prayer without a shred of evidence in their life, also known as, fruit. They still act, and think as they did before they said a prayer. As Children, we are expected to become like our adopting Father, by renewing our formerly perverted mind.

Do not be conformed to this world, but be transformed by the renewing of your mind... Romans 12:2

If the Word calls us children, then we must begin to think and act as Children of God, not Children of the Devil. If you have children, then you probably know how to love your children. If you've never had children, and you're reasonably normal, you should be able to figure out how you would treat your own kids, and how much you would love them.

For example, let's say you have a nine-year-old boy and he is outside playing basketball with his friends and he comes running in the house and says "Mom, I'm thirsty." Does he really have to beg you? "Can I go in the refrigerator and get a drink, please?" If he did, you would say, "Go get a drink. You are my son. Anything and everything I have is yours. Help yourself, make yourself at home, clean up after yourself, and don't make a mess."

If all of us are loved by The Father, including those who have not received Him, then how much more does Our Father love those who do believe? In Matthew 7, Jesus begins shedding some light on the Fathers heart towards us...

If you then, who are evil, know how to give good gifts to your children, how much more will your Father who is in Heaven give good things to those who ask him! Matthew 7:11

Now, what's particularly funny to me is the fact that he calls them evil to their face. The point is, that compared to God, we are evil and if we can love our own kids, how much more a loving God? David paints a beautiful picture of just how much our Father thinks about us in Psalm 139,

How precious to me are Your thoughts, O God, how vast is their sum! If I were to count them, they would outnumber the grains of sand. Psalm 139:17-18

We are the apple of His eye, and He has more thoughts towards us than there are grains of sand. Have you ever stopped to consider that? In Jeremiah 29, He says:

For I know the plans I have for you, declares the Lord, plans to prosper you and not to harm you, plans to give you hope and a future. Jeremiah 29:11

God is good, we serve a good God. He is our Father, Galatians 4:6 says, *Because you are sons, God sent the Spirit of His Son into our hearts, crying out, Abba, Father!* Abba in the Greek is Strong's #5 Abbá – Father, is used as a term of <u>tender endearment</u> by a beloved child, i.e.: in an <u>affectionate</u>, <u>dependent</u> relationship with their father, similar to daddy or papa. We need to grasp this concept, an understanding of the kind of relationship our Father wants with us. It is not like the Old Testament, where they were terrified. God is telling us that He wants us to see Him as our daddy. I want you to get this concept deep into your heart, and never let it go.

But here's the thing, we must choose to have this type of personal relationship with our Father. He is there for us, but it's up to us to pursue it. The closeness of our relationship is dependent upon us. James puts it so simply when he says,

> *Draw near to God, and he will draw near to you.* James 4:8

If we want a personal relationship with Him, He will have a personal relationship with us, and if we do not want a personal relationship with Him, He is not going to force Himself upon us. He is so loving and sweet that He gives us free will. His attitude towards us is that He wants to be with us, to love us and to bless us, but only if that is what we want, too. If we chose not to, He respects our decision, but no matter what, He will be there waiting for us, if and when we ever change our minds. Now, that I think about it, shouldn't we have this same attitude towards other people, as well.

> *He predestined us for adoption, to himself as sons through Jesus Christ.* Ephesians 1:5

Whether Children of God, or unbelievers, God will never stop loving any of us as long as we are alive. He will never get to the point of no return and say, "Enough is enough. I am done with them. They are hopeless. I don't love them anymore." People, even Children of God, do it often, but God never does it with us. People separate themselves from Him all the time, but He is never going to turn His back on us, because it is His desire that all creation get saved.

God our Savior, who desires all men to be saved and to come to the knowledge of the truth. For there is one God and one mediator between God and men, the man Christ Jesus.
1 Timothy 2:3-5

But to all who receive His gift of salvation, those who believe on the name of His Son, Jesus, the Word says that we are adopted. We are different than the people of the world. We are, also, different than the Jews. While they are, also, called Children of God, they have chosen to turn their back on Jesus. Their only saving grace is, *God is not a man that He should lie.* He made covenant with them and He will always keep up His end of the deal. We, believers in Jesus, are also children, but we are adopted children, and as a parent that has adopted a child, I can tell you from experience, that it is a significantly different relationship. Not only is there is a legal precedent that makes adoption a stronger, more binding legal obligation than that of natural children, but there is, also, an emotional bond that I cannot describe.

He predestined us for adoption as His sons through Jesus Christ, according to the good pleasure of His will, Eph. 1:5

I love all three of my kids and I'd gladly die for any one of them, but the relationship with my adopted son is special. I don't really know how to describe it. It's not like I love him more or that I would do any more or less, but it's like I want to prove my loyalty, because he's adopted. With my natural kids, I don't feel like I have to prove myself, I know they know, but it's so important to me that my adopted son believe I love him as my very own, that I'm likely to go the extra mile for him. FYI, I have only ever referred to him as my adopted son for the sake of making this point here. To me, he is just my son.

During the times of Jesus and Paul, it was not uncommon for a parent to sell his natural child or to give them in trade or use them to pay off a debt. However, an adopted child could not be sold or traded or used as chattel. The adopting parent had a stronger legal obligation to their adopted child than with their natural born children. The adopted child's rights could not be taken away, nor could they be given away.

When you are in Christ, you are adopted as sons of God through Christ Jesus. Whether male or female, believers are described as sons for a specific reason. The implication is that of a first born son, he will receive a greater inheritance than the younger son. As adopted sons of God, nothing can ever separate you from God's love, except you. Only you, can separate yourself, from the love of God, because you have the free will to choose to turn yourself back on Him.

It is impossible for those who have once been enlightened, who have tasted the Heavenly gift, who have shared in the Holy Spirit, who have tasted the goodness of the word of God and the powers of the coming age, and then have fallen away, to be restored again to repentance, because they themselves are crucifying the Son of God all over again and subjecting Him to open shame. Heb 6:4-6

The phrase, 'fall away,' here is Strong's #3895 /parapíptō ("fallen from a close position into the unbelieving and Godless ways of their old way of living"). It refers to a <u>close follower</u> of Christ, who becomes a defector. It suggests this person, at least at one time, was a believer and now they are behaving as though they are not. Sounds ridiculous, but it's actually more common than you think.

I struggled with this verse as it is very difficult to wrap my brain around. On the surface it appears like backsliders can never return to a saved state. However, we know that is not true, because people do it all the time, so what is Paul really saying here? Let us consider what Jesus said about forgiveness,

Then Peter came to Jesus and asked, Lord, how many times shall I forgive my brother who sins against me? Up to seven times? Jesus answered, I tell you, not just seven times, but seventy-seven times! Matthew 18:21-22

The point is not to say that we must forgive 1,400 times and that's it, but it's a number so ridiculous. Forgiveness has no end. God's never going to expect us to do something He's not willing to do Himself. If He expects us to have endless patience towards others, as long as we are alive, His patience towards us is endless, as well. That being the case, Paul cannot be implying that forgiveness and restoration are not available from God's end, so it must be something on our end.

I used to believe that Paul was saying it was impossible for someone who is enlightened, who has tasted the Heavenly gift, who has shared in the Holy Spirit, and tasted the goodness of the Word of God and the power of the age to come, to fall away. Anyone that could move in that power surely would not be so stupid as to go back to the vomit of the world. That's what I used to think, but now I know better, because I know people that have done just that and it blows me away. I used to think that no person on Earth could ever leave the power of God and return to the dregs of the Earth, but having been close to people who have done so, having watched their descent back into the world, has opened my eyes to this verse.

The biggest culprit for ones reasoning behind such a decent is the Once Saved Always Saved doctrine of demons. Satan had deceived them into thinking they are safe, because they are covered by grace, and therein, lies the problem and the explanation of this verse. It's impossible for them to be restored to repentance, because they had to fall for the false grace message in order to justify their worldly behavior in the first place. It's that same false grace hope that will prevent them from seeking repentance, because they don't think they need to. They think they're covered by grace, but they are not.

Paul says it perfectly in Galatians 5:

But if you are led by the Spirit, you are not under the Law. The works of the flesh are obvious: sexual immorality, adultery, and debauchery; drunkenness, revelries, idolatry and sorcery; hatred, discord, jealousy, and rage; rivalries, divisions, factions... Galatians 5:18-20

What nobody is willing to admit, what no preacher wants to tell his flock is this, "if you are led by the Spirit, you are **not** under the Law," however, IF YOU WALK IN THE FLESH **YOU ARE UNDER THE LAW** - NOT GRACE! If someone is exhibiting behavior described as "works of the flesh" as listed above, they are no longer under grace, but under the law. They are in serious trouble, but condemnation is not the purpose of this book, its repentance and restoration. If the Holy Spirit is convicting you as you read this, run don't walk. Run back to your first love, who is Jesus. As Jesus said repeatedly in Revelation 2 and 3, *Come back to your first love, repent and come back home to Me, or else. See what great love the Father has lavished on us, that we should be called children of God! And that is what we are.* 1 John 3:1

Now if we are children, then we are heirs, heirs of God and co-heirs with Christ... Romans 8:17

An heir is someone that is legally entitled to the property or rank of another upon death. We are Children of God, and in as much, we are children and heirs of all creation. Our God is above every God, the Most High God, the Lord God is our Father, our daddy. We are heirs to the throne. Everything the Father has, belongs to us. We stand in the lineage to receive everything that was passed down to Jesus, even His rank. We now walk as He walked in His Authority and power.

The earth and everything in it, the world and its inhabitants, belong to the LORD... Psalm 24:1

All that the Father has is Mine; therefore I said that He will take what is Mine and declare it to you John 16:15

God owns everything in the world, He owns it all and He gave it to Jesus, and Jesus said, *He will take what is mine and declare it to you.* What do we have then? We have everything. We have Authority over everything and the right to use it. Therefore, if everything belongs to God and we are heirs, then it only stands to reason that we will inherit everything the Father has which is everything. Unlike earthly heirs, we don't have to wait for someone to die to receive the benefit of it. Every promise, every gift, every benefit, and every blessing belongs to us now. Why then, do we not walk like children and talk like children and act like children? I suppose it's because we either do not know we are children who are heirs, or we do not understand what it really means to be a child who is an heir.

Suppose you were the only child of Bill Gates, and he had already informed you that everything he has would be passed down to you. One day you are having dinner with a friend and an old acquaintance comes to your table and begins harassing you. You see, this isn't just any old acquaintance, this is someone that antagonized you all through school for no reason at all. Let's suppose they finished their barrage by saying that you were completely worthless. Are you going to lose your cool? No! Will you feel the need to vehemently defend yourself? No! Why? Because you know who you are, and you know exactly how much you are worth. The entire premise they spewed is so ridiculous that you are likely to laugh in their face and shoo them away like an annoying little fly, because you know who you are and what your inheritance is.

Why is it then that we are fully capable of understanding our inheritance as an earthly heir, but we have problems believing our Heavenly Father when He says that we are co-heirs with Christ?

Now if we are children, then we are heirs, heirs of God and co-heirs with Christ. Romans 8:17

Yet, which is more real, the natural realm or the spiritual realm?

So, we do not look at the things which are seen, but on what is unseen. For what is seen is temporary, but what is unseen is eternal. 2 Cor. 4:18

The world we see around us is not the real world, it is akin to the matrix. In order for Children of God to rule and rein as heirs, they must get a full understanding of their Identity as children and heirs.

Ephesians 1:21 Paul says, *I pray that you will understand...* Stop! Slow your roll here. What? When I first saw this, it jumped off the page at me. Why would Paul be praying that we understand something unless we did not understand it? Furthermore, how important was it if Paul was going to pray we understand it? Let's read it again:

I pray that you will understand the incredible greatness of God's power, the same mighty power that raised Jesus from the dead and seated Him at God's right hand, in the Heavenly places, far above every principality, power and dominion and every name that is named, not only in this age, but also in the one to come and put everything under His feet. Eph. 1:21

Paul is trying to get us to understand the magnitude of the power of God that raised Jesus from the dead and seated him at the right hand of the Father. Further, Paul describes how this power has exalted Jesus above everything, all the angels, the demons and everything that has a name. To be far above indicates Authority over a thing, therefore, if it has a name, Jesus is in Authority over it. But the most intriguing part is when Paul says that everything was put under His feet. The term, "under His feet," is a Jewish idiom, which implies complete mastery or domination. Imagine a war, where one side had sticks and stones and the other had nuclear bombs. That would be considered complete domination. It's not even a contest. Anytime you read that something is under your feet, or that you step on it, or tread on it, that phrase implies that you completely dominate that thing. Another way to describe it, is to say that it is under your Authority.

Jesus is now head over everything. All principalities, all powers, everything the Devil has and anything he does, Jesus is now the master of it. He has Authority over it, therefore, Satan and all of His schemes must submit to the Authority of Jesus. It is not optional, He does not have a choice in the matter. It's the law. Then, in Ephesians Paul says,

God has raised us up with Christ and seated us with Him in the Heavenly realms in Christ Jesus... Ephesians 2:6

Remember, Paul was saying that he wanted us to understand the great power that raised Jesus from the dead. Then he says that God has raised us up with Christ Jesus and seated us with Him.

The Spirit of Him who raised Jesus from the dead lives in you. Rom. 8:11

This is what Paul was praying, that we understand that the same power, the same Authority that raised Jesus from the dead, now lives in us and is available to us as adopted children and co-heirs with Christ. Picture it, there is God, and there is Jesus seated at the right hand of God... and there we are, all snuggled up, right next to Jesus. Adoption has given us the privilege and honor of sitting on the throne with Jesus, because of what He did on the cross. It is a symbol of our identity and our Authority in Christ Jesus. We are as royalty, heirs to a Heavenly throne, to the Great God, the Lord God Almighty, the owner and creator of all things.

In Isaiah 52, Isaiah was prophesying and describing what was going to happen at the cross.

His appearance was so disfigured beyond that of any human being and His form marred beyond human likeness. Isa. 52:14

The Bible does not lie nor does it exaggerate, so when it says, *His appearance was so disfigured beyond that of any human being...* It is saying that no man in the history of the world has ever been tortured as bad as Jesus, not before, nor after. And when it says, *and His form marred beyond human likeness,* it is saying that the beating and torture Jesus endured, was so horrendous that he no longer looked like a human being on the cross. Anyone that has seen the film, The Passion, can attest to the gruesome scene in the courtyard where Jesus was scourged. There were several times that I had to look away. It was that horrible, but the way the text is written, the movie wasn't even close to the actual event.

But why? Why would God do that to Jesus? If Jesus was simply coming for our salvation, why would He have to be beaten like that? What did it have to do with salvation? Wasn't it enough for Him to just die for our sins? No, it wasn't, and the reason Jesus did not look like a human anymore to us, is because we did not look like what God created us to be. We had so taken on the image and likeness of Satan, that we no longer looked like Children of God. Jesus took our identity and He gave us His. It was an even exchange. You see, forgiveness was just the avenue, through which, He could transfer our rightful heritage back to us. If salvation was the only thing the cross had done for us, it would be a divine gift, but the cross accomplished way more than just salvation. It restored our position as Children in the Kingdom, and regained the Identity that Satan had stolen from us, the same Identity He's been hiding from us since the cross.

Instead of looking like children, we look like trash. We are hateful, because Satan is hateful. We are jealous, because Satan is jealous. We are depressed, because Satan is depressed. We are murderous, because Satan is a murderer. We are lustful, because Satan is full of lust. We are rebellious, because Satan was a rebel. We are rude, prideful, and selfish, because Satan is. Satan has successfully projected his disgusting, vile nature on mankind, but Jesus, by way of the cross, took Satan's grotesque nature, the spirit of this world, and exchanged it with His Holy Spirit.

That is why the Bible calls us the righteous of God in Christ Jesus. If we are "in Christ," we have the ability to take on all the characteristics of Jesus. As He is faithful, we are faithful. As He is gentle, kind, and considerate, so are we. We are encouraged and joyful, because He is. We now have the right and the ability to take all His beautiful qualities and personality traits, because He took away our ugliness on the cross. Just as Jesus took our sin and gave us His righteousness, so we could be saved, likewise. He took away our demonic identity and gave us His righteousness, so now we look like Him to the Father again. That is the essence of who you are. That is your Identity, your right to look like King Jesus.

Every evil, angry, lustful, hateful, depressed, selfish, anxious, unforgiving, and murderous characteristic of the Devil, was taken away that day on the cross by Jesus, so we could be a reflection of our King to this dying world. As Jesus loves unconditionally, so can we, as He forgives, so can we, as He is compassionate, so are we, as He is full of grace and mercy, so are we. No longer do we have to behave like the enemy of our Father, but now we can model our King. Lastly, the cross gained us back our Authority. The one thing Satan never imagined was that He would lose. The most valuable thing he possessed, Authority, has now come back to the Children of God by way of adoption, the rightful heirs that understand their true Identity.

The Identity of a believer can be difficult for many who were physically or emotionally abused by their parents, or whoever raised them. However, one of the greatest benefits of understanding your identity as a Child of God and as an heir, is that you become aware that your childhood, your parents, your past mistakes, your race, your hair texture or skin color, as well as, any negative or traumatic events that formed or shaped your personality and belief system, do not determine who you are. Your identity is and should always be based upon who your Heavenly Father is, what your Lord and Savior Jesus did for you on the cross, and what He says about you. The Devil is a liar and He's going to lie to you about you, so it is imperative that you get the Word in you and find out what your Father says and thinks about you.

But one thing I do: Forgetting what is behind and straining toward what is ahead. Philippians 3:12

Paul instructs us to forget the past. We are not supposed to focus on what happened to us, but to look expectantly towards our new birth in Christ. Why? Because Satan will use your past against you. He will take all your past mistakes and throw them in your face in an attempt to gain a foothold for a guilty and shameful spirit. If you entertain the guilty (demonic) spirit and give Authority to the shameful (demonic) spirit to stay, it will try to usher in depression. If you welcome depression, that demonic spirit will try to usher in suicide, because death is Satan's ultimate goal. Therefore, you should stay away from your past. Just consider that person dead and you are a new creation in Christ Jesus.

Therefore, if any man be in Christ, he is a new creature: old things are passed away; behold, all things are become new. 2 Corinthians 5:17

I, particularly, like the way Paul put it in Philippians:

Nothing is as wonderful as knowing Christ Jesus my Lord. I have given up everything else and count it all as garbage. All I want is Christ. Phil. 3:11

Everything we knew, all that we did and all that we were before we made Jesus our Lord, is to be considered as garbage when compared to the life we now live, through the finished work of the cross. That is why Paul instructs us to:

Throw off your old sinful nature and your former way of life, which is corrupted by lust and deception. Ephesians 4:22

Very early in my walk with Christ, my friends, Joe and Susan Hilyard, two of the most influential people in my salvation, took me to my first prayer meeting. A young woman, mid 30's was wailing on and on about how her husband had left her to raise her three kids by herself. After an hour of listening intently to her plight and ministering the Word to her, the pastor finally prayed with her and began the study. Immediately after we finished, the same woman broke into another, oh poor me pity party, as she lay across his couch sobbing, "The scars, the scars." We hung out for another 30 minutes, in which, she wailed and cried, until we finally just left. As we got in the car, my friend's wife, Susan, turned around and asked me, "So what did you think of that?"

Let me remind you that I was a new Christian. I had no idea how this thing worked. In my mind, I'm thinking, Is this the way a Christian behaves? I don't know, but it sure didn't look normal, and to be honest, the whole thing really turned me off. I'm generally not melodramatic, so if that is what Christianity is supposed to look like, I'm not impressed. So my response to her was, "The scars, the scars!" and we all burst into laughter. Then Susan said, "You are correct, that was ridiculous behavior. She really doesn't want to be free of her misery. It's her comfort zone."

I would learn over the years, that some Christians really don't want a solution to their problems. Some just want to embrace them and wallow in them. It's the attention they desire. They love the attention and sympathy Christians will give them through prayers and such. As long as their problem remains, they have the attention they crave. Once again, it comes back to identity, because had she known who she was and the price that was paid for her, she would have let go of her past and forged ahead in her new life as a believer. Until we learn to let go of our past, God cannot bless us with an awesome new future. We will simply go around and around that mountain, until we learn to let go and press onward.

The value of knowing and understanding one's identity is perfectly displayed in the biblical account of the Seven Sons of Sceva in Acts 19. As was Paul's modus operandi, he entered a town and began performing miracles: raising the dead, healing the sick, casting out demons, etc. After he had gotten their attention by the power of the Holy Spirit, he would then minister about Christ and The Crucifixion. Sceva, a wealthy, prominent man of the territory, had seven sons who must have watched Paul performing these awesome miracles and wanted in on the act. These were children of privilege, and you know the pompous attitude that privileged kids of wealthy parents have. Surely they must have said to themselves, "We might have notoriety and money, but this thing Paul is doing is way better."

The Bible describes how they came across a man with a demon and they said to the demon, "Come out of him in the name of Jesus that Paul preaches." Now, the demon doesn't do anything right away. You see, he must qualify them first. Finally, the demon responds, "Jesus I know, Paul I know, who are you?" In other words, he was saying, "Do you know who you are? Are you a Child of the Lord God, an heir to the throne, able to cast me to the pit of Hell, never to return again? Do you know? Are you one of them? Because, if you are not a Child, a co-heir with Jesus, like Paul is, or if you are a child, but don't know that you have Authority over me... well then, I'm fixin' to unleash a can of whoop-butt on you, like you've never seen before." Apparently, the boys had no clue who they were, because the story goes on to say that the demon beat them nearly to death, stripped them naked and chased them down the street.

Identity is the first lesson a new believer should learn. Churches should have Bible studies designed for different levels of believers, but especially, new believers. New believers need to spend time learning who they are in Christ and how the Kingdom of God operates, before they learn anything else.

Christians that understand their Identity are less likely to fall away and go back to the world. Christians who understand their Identity are less likely to get offended, hold a grudge or get in a fight. Christians who understand their Identity are more likely to walk in love, work hard at their job, and be fair bosses to their employees. Christians who understand their Identity are less likely to lie, cheat, or steal. Christians who understand their Identity are more likely to be kind, helpful, and generous. Christians who understand their Identity are more likely to be faithful to their spouse, loving to their kids, and respectful to their parents.

Why? Because part of knowing your Identity is knowing the world no longer revolves around you. You are not the center of the Universe, regardless of what your mamma told you, bless her heart. As a child of God, everything you do should be done like you were doing it for Jesus.

Whatever you do, do it enthusiastically, as something done for the Lord and not for men, Colossians 3:23

When a Christian understands their Identity, their entire attitude will change from a place of selfishness to a place of giving. It's no longer what you can get from the world, but what you can give. They look for people to bless and places to volunteer. This is a lost, hurt, and dying world and it needs help. Everyone needs prayer, whether they admit it, or not.

Think about it like this, only one out of every 100 people you pass everyday might be saved. Everyone else is dead already and needs to come alive. Be the person that opens their eyes of understanding by sharing the saving work of Jesus on the cross. Tell them who they were created to be, Children of the Most High God.

Once you learn who you are as a Child of God, you have to tell others. If you really understand your Identity, then you understand the value of it and you will want everyone to know who they were created to be. If you truly are a Child of God and you understand your Identity, how can you, in good conscience, keep it to yourself? Christianity is the ultimate networking marketing program, peddling the most valuable product in the world... eternal life. Turn someone on to it today.

Chapter Four

Authority of a Believer: Leg 2 of The Altar of Love

I've spent a lot of time studying and researching the Authority of believers. And most of the time, when we should be demanding and commanding that things be done, we sheepishly ask our Father to do the things for us; things He put in our Authority to do. What if, the reason we have not received our prayers, our miracles, our healing, and the end to our trials is because God is waiting for us to assume the Authority He has already given to us.

Children of God, who understand that they have been adopted into the Royal Family as co-heirs with Christ, are the perennial Authority here on Earth. As in Exodus with Moses, God uses a child to carry out His plan, 'On Earth as it is in Heaven.' Have you ever wondered why bad things happen to good Christians, or why believers many times end up broken, sick and defeated, and never know why? Sometimes, when taking people through The Altar of Love, I find that they are angry at God, because they've been standing and believing for something for years, sometimes even decades and its only gotten worse. They've hardened their heart towards God, because it just doesn't make any sense. They say, "I prayed day and night and I get nothing, no answer, no healing, no resolution, not even a word, nothing."

We can pretend that Satan's not there, but Jesus himself said,

> *The thief only comes to steal, kill, and destroy. I came that they may have life, and may have it abundantly.* John 10:10

I am a man of power and great strength. I have trained in the art of combat and fighting skills for four decades, so that, if I were to get in a fight with a 200 lb. man, I will win every time. If, however, that man is an officer of the law, with a badge and a gun, I will come out on the losing end. You see, he can call for backup, and if he has the misfortune to tangle with me, he's going to need it. As an officer of the law, he has the total resources of the State of Texas at his disposal. He has the court, the judge, and the jail, and while I will win the battle, I'll certainly lose the war. That, my friend is the awesome power of Authority, and once Authority is attained, it is my advice that you do whatever it takes to maintain it. NEVER, EVER, UNDER ANY CIRCUMSTANCES, GIVE UP YOUR AUTHORITY, because within it lies the miracle power and backing of the living God. The power within Authority is so great that nothing above, below, or on Earth can overcome it.

Now to Him who is able to do infinitely more than all we ask or imagine, according to His power that is at work within us…
Ephesians 3:20

The word power is translated from Strong's concordance #1411 "dunamis," and it is where the English language gets the word dynamite from. The short definition of 'dunamis' is: miraculous power, mighty strength. This miracle power that Paul is referring to, is like the power of dynamite and it only belongs to adopted Children of God, who understand their Identity and walk in Authority.

And God blessed them (Adam & Eve). And God said to them, Be fruitful and multiply and fill the earth and subdue it, and have dominion over the fish of the sea and over the birds of

69

the Heavens and over every living thing that moves on the earth. Genesis 1:28

In Psalm 8, David confirms that we were created to have dominion when he said,

For You (God) have made him (man) a little lower than the angels, And You have crowned him with glory and honor. You have made him to have dominion over the works of Your hands; You have put all things under his feet. Psalm 8:4-6

Let's take this apart and let the Holy Spirit show us something. David begins with, *For You (God) have made him (man) a little lower than the angels.* The meaning of the word lower in this context (needy); humans were made needier than the angels. How so? The angels were created to be self-sufficient, in that, they did not need God to survive. We, on the other hand, need God to sustain us. We need God for the very air we breathe, and without Him, we would surely die. Not the angels though. One third of them fell away and they seem to be doing quite well, for the time being, anyway. Humans, however, are lost without God. We were designed specifically to need Him, as well as, to fellowship with Him. Without him, we are lonely, desperate, depressed, and even suicidal.

It is a well known fact that most suicides happen to rather wealthy, successful people. Why? Success, with its large bank accounts, big houses, and fancy cars and toys, can't make you happy. We were created to have a relationship with God. The angels didn't need Him to survive, but we do. Without him, we are hopelessly lost. Only Jesus can fill the void in our hearts. Success always leads to one question, Is this it? Is this all there is to life? I have need of nothing, and I'm still not happy. Satan knows that most people can't handle it and feeds these negative thoughts with lies, If nothing makes me happy, what's the point? Why not just end it now?

Not poor people, they always have something to live for, whether they marry the spouse of their dreams, land a better job, or win the lottery. It might be a false hope, but it is a hope none-the-less. It's that hope that keeps them alive. For most, money is a curse. Bad decisions and sin cause trials, and money only postpones our need to deal with the sinful nature. It truly is the root of all kinds of evil and will severely stunt your spiritual growth. Who needs faith when you have money? Money is never a solution; it can only mask the symptoms of the cause.

Next, David says, **And You have crowned him with glory and honor.** This is an illustration of our Royal Heritage, our place in the Kingdom, which speaks to our Identity as Children and co-heirs with Christ, seated in Heavenly places with the Father and our King Jesus. Servants are not crowned with glory and honor, only those in the lineage of royalty are. This prophetic passage of David perfectly confirms The Altar of Love, as he goes on to describe our Authority, **You have made him to have dominion over the works of Your hands; He made us to have dominion,** which implies that we were created for the very purpose of ruling and reining over the things that God created with his hands. If God created it, we are supposed to rule over it, to dominate it. God intended for us to have dominion from the very beginning. It was our job and our responsibility, to dominate the works of His hands.

Genesis describes man's God-given dominion to rule and rein over the Earth. In Psalms, David confirms that we had this

Authority called, Dominion. However, when Adam and Eve sinned, they handed their Authority, their Dominion, over to Satan. With His new found Authority stolen from mankind, Satan had all but sealed our fate. For the next 4,000 years Satan wields this Authority, this Dominance, over man with an iron fist. The fate of the world looks bleak. Luke 4 gives us an account of Satan bragging about his Authority to Jesus.

Then the Devil led Him up to a high place and showed Him in an instant all the kingdoms of the world. I will give You Authority over all these kingdoms and all their glory, he said. For it has been relinquished to me, and I can give it to anyone I wish. So if You worship me, it will all be Yours. Luke 4:5

With confidence, Satan tells Jesus how it is. He has Authority and He can give it to whomever He wishes. This is a correct statement, and proven by the fact that Jesus does not argue with Satan or set him straight. Remember, while God does own everything, He gave the legal right, the lease of the Earth to Adam, but Adam, through sin, handed it to Satan. Therefore, what Satan is saying here is 100% true. He did have the Authority and He could have given it to whomever He wished. Personally, I don't believe Satan would have ever given his Authority away, knowing how valuable it is. No, He is a liar and He had no intentions of handing over Authority to Jesus, or anyone, for that matter. But God is a genius, and He figured out a way to come here Himself and save us from that monster, the old red dragon. In Psalm 22, David prophesied what would happen on the cross 500 years before it ever happened, and well before crucifixion was even invented.

My God, my God, why have you forsaken me? Why are you so far from saving me, from the words of my groaning?

72

O my God, I cry by day, but you do not answer, and by night, but I find no rest.

Yet you are holy, enthroned on the praises of Israel.

In you our fathers trusted; they trusted, and you delivered them.

To you they cried and were rescued; in you they trusted and were not put to shame.

But I am a worm and not a man, scorned by mankind and despised by the people.

All who see me mock me; they make mouths at me; they wag their heads; He trusts in the Lord; let him deliver him; let him rescue him, for he delights in him!

Yet you are he who took me from the womb; you made me trust you at my mother's breasts.

On you was I cast from my birth, and from my mother's womb you have been my God.

Be not far from me, for trouble is near, and there is none to help. Many bulls encompass me; strong bulls of Bashan surround me; they open wide their mouths at me, like a ravening and roaring lion.

I am poured out like water, and all my bones are out of joint; my heart is like wax; it is melted within my breast; my strength is dried up like a potsherd, and my tongue sticks to my jaws; you lay me in the dust of death.

For dogs encompass me; a company of evildoers encircles me; they have pierced my hands and feet.

I can count all my bones, they stare and gloat over me;

they divide my garments among them, and for my clothing they cast lots.

But you, O Lord, do not be far off! O you my help, come quickly to my aid. Psalm 22

Once Jesus allowed himself to be crucified, He was taken to Hell where He put a nasty whoopin' on the Devil.

When He had disarmed the rulers and authorities, He made a public display of them, having triumphed over them through Him. Col. 2:15

The phrase, 'Public Display,' describes the sadistic way Romans treated newly conquered kingdoms. At the public display, the Romans would force all the people of the kingdom to attend. Using a large trailer similar to the kind used in modern day parades, they would take the king and queen and any other immediate members of the royal family, strip them naked and parade them, for all to see. If that wasn't humiliating enough, the Romans would beat and torture them instilling fear and intimidation into all the people of the land. In other versions of the Bible, a public display, is also translated as an 'open show' or a 'public spectacle,' and that is what Jesus did to Satan when Jesus was taken illegally to Hell. Jesus, the King of Kings, entered Hell like a lion, grabbed Satan by the throat, and dragged him around for all the demons to see, demonstrating His power and regained Authority. The New English Version Bible describes the event much more accurately, saying,

He stripped the rulers and authorities [of their power]
and made a public spectacle of them as he celebrated
His victory in Christ. Colossians 2:15

The cross gained us back the three things that Adam gave away: our Salvation, our Identity, and our Authority. Authority was the one thing Satan never imagined he would lose. Authority, the most valuable thing Satan possessed is gone for good... or is it?

God's plan of the cross was brilliant, and He turned the tables on Satan as Authority was ripped from His wretched claws and given to back to the rightful heirs, the Children of God, who were created to have it from the beginning. This Dominion, this awesome power known as Authority, is not for just anybody and it must not be taken lightly. It only applies to heirs, the adopted children that have crucified the flesh and chosen to live for Christ at all costs, and only when they invoke the name of Jesus. For this Authority is a power so great, that it can part waters, stop time, slay giants, enable one man to defeat a thousand, raise the dead, cleanse a leper, make the blind see, the lame walk, and demons shudder and flee.

With this power called Authority, we become the sheriff. We have the badge, we have the gun, we have the backup forces known as the Angels of God, we run the court and the jail, and we are the judge, the jury and the executioner. No wonder why Satan wanted Authority so badly. With it, He had regained all the power He lost when He was evicted from Heaven. To the believers who understand that they are Children of God by reason of adoption, Authority has now been purchased for us by the blood of Jesus. Only Children of God, who act, think, and behave, like heirs to the King, are eligible to access this Authority. They are children who walk in the spirit and not in the flesh, and who love their eternal God more than the temporary pleasures of this dying world.

Now, before we continue, there is one thing that must be made perfectly clear, the Word says, **God is not a man that He should lie, and Let God be true and every man a liar.** It is impossible for God to lie and Jesus never exaggerated when He walked the Earth. He never came back to His disciples and said, "Well... ya know, I didn't really mean to say that, what I meant was..." If He said it, He meant it. With that in mind, listen carefully to this next thing He says, for if you get this, your life will never be the same.

> **Behold, I have given you Authority to tread on serpents and scorpions, and over all the power of the enemy, and nothing shall hurt you.** Luke 10:19

Behold, He said**, I have given you Authority to tread on...** The Authority that Jesus regained when he made a 'public display' of Satan, has been transferred back to us, the rightful heirs. Authority has come back to its rightful home. Next, Jesus says, "to tread on," and if you recall, that phrase means to dominate something. Jesus is saying that He has given us the Authority to completely Dominate, to have total mastery over a thing. But over what? What has Jesus given us mastery over? Jesus has made us masters over serpents and scorpions, which is really nothing more than a metaphor for Satan and the demon forces. Therefore, Jesus is saying, **Behold, I give you Authority, the legal right to dominate with complete mastery over Satan and the demon forces!**

Remember, you're the sheriff now. You've got the gun, the badge, and the jail. Satan is the criminal being hunted by the law, running scared and hiding... or He should be! In fact, let's take this analogy of the sheriff a bit farther. Suppose you were a sheriff, and a citizen within your precinct calls you to report a break-in at their home. You take the call, acknowledge the crime, hang up the phone, grab a donut, change the channel of the TV, kick your feet up on the desk, and pretend the call never happened. Is that the way a sheriff does his job? No, at the very least, the sheriff must be reactive, he must pursue the enemy, and bring him to justice. Let me offer some advice here... the best defense against the enemy we are facing, is to be proactive, not reactive.

If we are reacting to things that Satan is doing in our lives, then we are always working from behind, always needing a miracle to get us back to normal. On the other hand, if we learn to become proactive we control and determine our destiny, not the other way around. However, because we live in a fallen world, and because we are affected by the sin of people connected to us, there will be times we have to be reactive. But the more proactive we are, the less reactive we will need to be. Taking Authority over every situation and covering ourselves and our loved ones in prayer are just two ways to be proactive, but neither is the best way. The best way to be proactive is to never give up your Authority in the first place, because without Authority, Satan has no legal right to bring accusation against you, or do you harm. Yes, you can actually give up your Authority and I will discuss this in great detail, shortly.

This Authority to Dominate is a most profound and amazing revelation, but it's just the tip of the iceberg, because it only gets better. After Jesus tells us that we now have Authority over Satan and the demon forces, He describes the actual extent of our Authority when He says, ***And over all the power of the enemy!*** If we have Authority over all the power of the enemy, how much power does the enemy have over us? Nothing! Satan has officially been neutered by Jesus and stripped of all his power for a second time. As remarkable as that is, Jesus goes on to say, ***and nothing shall hurt you.***

Do you see it? Do you see what He did here? In His Authority, Jesus has made us like actual super humans. Think about it. He isn't lying, because He can't lie, He doesn't exaggerate, and He just said that nothing can hurt you. If nothing can hurt you, what in the world are you supposed to be afraid of? **Nothing!** If nothing can hurt you, there's nothing to fear. If nothing can hurt us, we essentially become Superman in a world without kryptonite.

There's Superman, walking across a street and a semi loaded down with cinder blocks, going 100 miles per hour is just about to hit him and his last thought is... that poor driver, he's going to get hurt. Why? Because nothing can hurt Superman. If Jesus just said that nothing can hurt us, how are we any different than Superman? We're not!

Since we are like Supermen and Superwomen now, what can we compare Satan to? Satan is like Batman. He's got lots of fancy gadgets, like his Bat Belt and his Batmobile, but we have the ultimate superpower, because we have **Authority**. All Satan has now are parlor tricks and lies. In Matthew 18, Jesus begins to explain some of the benefits of Authority.

I will give you the keys of the kingdom of Heaven, and whatever you bind (prevent, cause to cease) on earth shall be bound in Heaven, and whatever you loose (to allow, to permit) on earth shall be loosed in Heaven. Matthew 18:18

This verse shows us how Authority works. To bind means to stop, to prevent, to restrict, to cease and desist. To loose means to send on your behalf, to allow, to assist and support you. Therefore, if I bind the works, powers and plans of the enemy that is attacking me in an area of my life, then the Lord Jesus is there to stop that thing the enemy was attempting to do to me. If we bind it on Earth, He will do it, on our behalf, from Heaven. Let's say you are praying for someone struggling with severe depression. You can bind the spirit of depression and loose peace, joy, comfort, and the mind of Christ. You bind the thing that is afflicting, and loose what is needed or lacking.

When we assume Authority, Jesus backs us up with all the power and resources of Heaven. Satan is a spiritual being, but we are natural, so we can't exactly put him in a headlock and make him submit, but Jesus can. We don't do it. Jesus does it, on our behalf, but only when we walk like Jesus, and talk like Jesus, and think like Jesus, and act like Jesus. Does that mean we have to be perfect? Oh, heck no!

> *If any man says they have no sin, he is a liar and the truth is not in him.* 1 John 1:8

However, if you walk like the Devil, and talk like the Devil, and think like the Devil, and act like the Devil... well, you know the old saying, "If it walks like a duck, sounds like a duck, and looks like a duck... it's a duck." Jesus said, *A tree is known by its fruit.*

With this Authority comes great power, but with great power and Authority comes much responsibility to use your new superpower on behalf of your Father in Heaven. You are no longer living selfishly. You are not here for your own pleasure, but for His good pleasure. Because you were purchased by the blood of Jesus, you don't own 'you' anymore. Paul referred to himself as a bondservant on multiple occasions. A bondservant is a slave. Paul said he was a slave for Jesus and he was mighty proud of it. Never forget that your enemy roams about like a roaring lion, seeking whom he may devour. The key word here is 'may,' because he can only devour you if you let him, and he devours you by stealing your **Authority from you and assuming your rightful position.**

God has highly exalted Jesus, and bestowed on Him the name which is above every name, so that at the name of Jesus **EVERY KNEE WILL BOW,** *of those who are in Heaven and on earth and under the earth.* Phil. 2:10

Bowing is akin to acquiescence or to recognize and submit to ones Authority. Therefore, every name that is named must submit to the Authority of the adopted children who invoke the name of Jesus. Cancer is a name, schizophrenia is a name, multiple sclerosis is a name, etc. If it has a name, it must submit, it does not have a choice; it cannot decide not to go, and it's not debatable unless you have given it your Authority to stay. If you have given Satan your Authority, not only does He have the legal right to enter, but He does not have to leave, either. All the rebuking in the world makes no difference, because the awesome power of Authority is real, it's legal, and it will either work for you or against you. It's up to you.

This Superpower called Authority is the legal right to cast out demons, heal the sick, raise the dead, speak words of knowledge and prophesy, and is the power that our King died on the cross to acquire for us, is ours to use as children and heirs, unless we give it away. We can and do, give our Authority away daily. You see, just like Adam, we can hand our Authority back to the Devil, in a variety of ways. Christians, who do not know they have Authority, give their Authority away. Believers who know about Authority, but never learned how to use it, give their Authority away. Children of God, who know what Authority is and how to use it, but are too lazy or afraid to pick a fight with the enemy, give their Authority away. By doing nothing, we give our Authority away.

These are just some of the awesome lessons that the Lord was teaching me in The Altar of Love, regarding Authority:

1) He revealed to me just how amazing and powerful this thing called Authority was.

2) The things we do and do not do, that Satan uses against us to take our Authority away.

3) How to get it back and how not to give it away again.

Before we go there, let us finish learning everything that Authority enables us to do, as co-heirs with Christ.

Now, I've been reading and studying my Bible for decades and I never saw this before, but when I did, it changed my life.

And he called the twelve together and gave them power and Authority over all demons and to cure diseases. Luke 9:1

So then, who has the Authority to cure diseases? We do! And let us carefully consider the exact meaning of Authority. If God has given Authority to us, it is ours to assume. Children that have been given Authority, also, have the responsibility to assume it. With Authority, comes great abilities and power, and if God has given us this amazing gift, He expects us to use it. Furthermore, He is not going to undermine our Authority. He is not going to do something He has given us the Authority to do. If Authority has been given to us to heal, it is our responsibility to heal and it is an insult to God for us to blame Him when we are sick and do not get healed. We beg and plead with God for the healing that never came, the healing that was always within our power to perform in the first place, because we were the ones with the Authority to do it, in the name of Jesus.

If you purchased a nail salon as a business venture, but realized that, not only were you not good at it, but you hated doing it. However, it is a good business and it makes a substantial profit, so you decide to hire a manager to run it for you. One day the manager calls you and says, "I'm out of supplies." As the owner, your response is, "You are the manager, manage the business. Otherwise, I'll hire someone that can." Think about it, if you have to do the job that you are paying them to do, why do you need them? God will not do anything that He has given us the Authority to do. Mainly, Authority is a lawful transfer of power and if He does it, He is breaking the law of Dominion. God is a righteous God and He breaks no laws, not even His own. He must follow the law, as well, and you can bet that Satan is there watching to see if God does break the law, because if God were to break one of His laws, Satan would have legal right to God's throne.

God has blessed us with Authority, and by law. He, too, is obligated to follow it. How many Christians have gotten angry at God for not healing them or coming to their rescue and blaming Him for all the misfortune in their life when all the while it was within their Authority to do for themselves? How embarrassed will they be when they stand before God and He shows them they were angry with him for something they didn't do? Millions upon millions of Christians have cursed God and fallen away, because of this very problem. I know this, because I witness it almost every time I take an Altar of Love case. This is what Jesus meant when He said, *My people perish for lack of knowledge.* It's the Authority you don't assume, that may destroy you.

Authority, that we either do not know we have, do not know how to use, are too lazy or afraid to use, which gives the Devil the legal right to kill, steal, and destroy us. Let's consider this from another angle, if I offered to give you $10,000 as a one-time gift, or I offered to give you a business that made $10,000 a week, which would you prefer? If you were wise, you'd take the business. Likewise, is the Authority given to us by God. He could have made it, so that we had to approach Him for every single request, but instead, He gave us the Authority and ability to do it ourselves. Instead of having to petition God for every little thing, we can, in our Authority, do it ourselves, in the name of Jesus.

You have to admit, it's waaaay better this way, but it takes a level of maturity. The church has no business teaching prosperity, until it first teaches maturity. Unless a Christian is fully matured in their Identity, their Authority, their ability to carefully control their tongue and walk in Love, unless they get this thing called The Altar of Love, money would only destroy them.

When I was a child, I spoke like a child, I thought like a child, I reasoned like a child. When I became a man, I gave up childish ways. 1 Cor. 13:11

We must first become mature, adult believers before we ever consider being worthy Stewards of vast sums of money. This is the brilliant deception behind the prosperity message. It's like giving the keys of a Corvette to a 9 year old boy and not even warning him to be careful. He'll be dead before the day is done, because the power and temptation to test the limits of the speed is beyond their ability to control it. Maturity should come before prosperity.

This is confirmed by Jesus in Mark 4:18, the parable of the sower. He said, *Still others are like the seeds sown among the thorns. They hear the word, but the cares of this life, the deceitfulness of wealth, and the desire for other things come in and choke the word, and it becomes unfruitful.*

We see here, that wealth is a deceitful tool of the Devil to choke the Word that is in us, so that it becomes unfruitful. "So what?" you say. "What's the danger in that?" It's a slippery slope, because when the Word is choked, people begin making compromises in the decisions of their life. Satan will introduce other influences to further confuse and conflate circumstances and situations until they have all but gone back to the world. It's a slow desensitization, like boiling a frog, that drags us into a place where Satan can destroy us. Why? Because he's afraid that one day we just might get this thing called Authority and destroy his kingdom. Wealth is just one of Satan's tools to derail us before we understand our Authority.

Paul knew the prosperity gospel was going to be a problem 2,000 years ago in 1 Timothy, when he said,

For the love of money is the root of all kinds of evil. By craving it, some have wandered away from the faith and pierced themselves with many sorrows. 1 Timothy 6:10

This saying is much deeper than Christians have ever considered. The term, 'pierced themselves,' is quite interesting. Pierced, comes from the Greek word peripeiró, (per- ee-pi'-ro), Strong's #4044. The Definition: I put on a spit; I pierce, wound deeply. It is likened to taking a piece of meat, piercing it through with a skewer and slow roasting it over an open fire. The implication of the saying that Satan will use money to slowly desensitize you, so he can kill you and eat you. With money, he will steal everything you hold dear and destroy all you have accomplished in the Kingdom of God. Therefore, before you seek riches, seek maturity, seek your Identity, seek your Authority, seek the ability to use your words properly and walk in love daily.

Ignorance is not an excuse either. We cannot argue and say, "But that's not fair, I didn't know I had Authority." We are expected to study to show ourselves approved. We are expected to assume Authority, whenever and wherever, it has been given to us by our Father. God knows we are here with a monster and He did not leave us here without the weapons we need to be victorious. God is so awesome. He understands that Satan is a narcissistic, egotistical, maniacal, sociopath and He's surrounded by hoards of equally sadistic demons, whose main goal is to kill, steal and destroy the Children of the Lord God.

Therefore, God has not left us here without the power and ability to utterly destroy the works of the Devil. When a believer understands his Identity and walks in his Authority, he is an unbeatable force for good in the Kingdom of God. That is exactly what Paul did. He simply did as Jesus did, because like Jesus, Paul knew who he was and the awesome power of Authority he had at his disposal.

After a few months of taking people through The Altar of Love as a form of deliverance and healing, I received an email from a woman desperate for help. Before we begin, I asked her to make me several lists:

1) Anything and everything that she did involving the occult, ie.: ouija boards, tarot cards, palm reading, spirit summoning, crystals, meditation, etc.

2) List all people/relationships with people that may have been involved with the occult, witchcraft, etc.

3) Sin, including, but not limited to, sexual sin, drug and alcohol use

4) Personality disorders, lust, greed, selfishness, rebellion, etc.

5) List all ailments and diseases

6) Sub-lists of all the symptoms of each ailment and disease

Let me make one thing perfectly clear, I do not want them confessing their sin to me. I am not God, and I don't really want to know it, but if they do it apart from me, they must follow the process in order to get deliverance and take

Authority away from the spirits that gained entry through the sinful behavior. This part can be embarrassing, and I get it, but sometimes they are past the shame. It's their call, I'm just there to serve. Being an adult, and having done many such cases, nothing really surprises me any longer, not like it did in the beginning, at least.

On several occasions, however, I noticed the confessing person become too graphic about their sexual exploits and immediately I shut the conversation and the case down. Within the hour I noticed a change in my personality, aggravation, impatience, and the like. It was Satan trying to pass onto me some demonic spirit, because of what I was doing. Immediately I would assume Authority and cast that thing to the pit of Hell, never to return, and immediately I'd be back to normal. These things are very subtle and you have to know your own personality. It, also, helps to have a spiritual partner to keep you accountable. You have to be sober, and you better be vigilant to do this job.

The very first thing I do after we go through The Altar of Love teaching, is to go through the list of occult activity. I did a case once where a woman had three pages of sicknesses, ailments and diseases, as well as, various symptoms that went with each. I spent the first hour teaching her about her Identity, her Authority, the Power of her Words and how to walk in Love. There were so many illnesses and symptoms that it took us an additional three hours to get through them all. When it came time to address occult activity, she insisted that she had none in her history. She claimed that she was saved at the age of four, raised in a spirit-filled home, her parents were evangelists, and she was surrounded by Christians her entire life. Like most, she backslid during college, where she engaged in fornication, but was restored to the faith upon marriage.

For the last 30 years, she has been serving the Lord without wavering. I tried to get her to go through the occult section, anyway, but she indignantly insisted there was nothing, so we passed it up and went straight to sin. After completing her lists, we began to address all her sicknesses, diseases, and ailments. One by one, as soon as, we took back Authority and commanded that thing to go, it went. Four and a half hours into the case, she is completely healed, or so we thought. This woman, who had been just about bed ridden for a decade was joyfully moving about, pain free.

Every symptom, every pain, every ailment was completely gone. I asked her to put me on speakerphone and try to find pain in her body. For the first time in years, she was pain free. She begins dancing and yelling with joy. I'm trying to get her attention, to get her back on the phone to talk to me, but she's so happy about her new pain free body that she's not hearing me. Finally, I get her attention, "Hey, talk to me," I said. "What? What? I'm fine, everything is awesome," she said. "No," I said, "I want you to go through every body part, one-by-one and tell me how it feels." "I'm fine, I'm fine," she said, "Except for this little sore spot in my lower left back, but it's nothing, I can barely feel it." Immediately, I knew that was not supposed to be there. "No, I said, that's not right, let's take care of it." She tried to talk me out of it, but I insisted. I began speaking to her back, taking Authority over it, when suddenly, I heard her scream, and say, "It just moved to the center of my spine and feels like a knife in my back." It must have been painful, because she began to cry.

I originally began this session with her while I was at work, but sensing that we were almost done, I was doing this part while driving home. "No worries," I said, "We'll get this thing." Once again, I began taking Authority over this obvious spirit and commanded it to go in the name of Jesus. This time, she let out a terrifying scream and said it had moved into her shoulder. She said the pain was getting worse each time we tried to evict it. Now, she's frightened. "It's okay, It's okay," I reassured her, "Lets double team this thing. You pray in tongues and I'll take Authority." We begin. She is bombarding it in the spirit and I'm assuming Authority in English and this time she let out a blood curdling scream, unlike anything I'd heard before. This time, she said it had moved into her jaw, and felt like she got hit with a sledge hammer in the face.

Now I'm freaking out, because this is way beyond anything I had experienced to date. I'm not shaken, just confused and she's wailing and screaming now, "Help me, help me!" As I pulled into my driveway, I told her that I just arrived home and I wanted to go inside and pray about what to do. She screamed, "Oh no don't, don't you leave me, do not hang up on me." She's desperate, so I reassured her I was not going anywhere, but I needed to regroup and ask the Holy Spirit what to do. I had no clue what I needed to do, but I wasn't about to tell her that. As far as she knew, I knew exactly what I was doing.

I went into my bedroom and sat on the bed and began to pray in the spirit, when suddenly I heard the word, "Witchcraft." Remembering how indignant she acted when I tried to take her through the occult section of The Altar of Love process, I said, "I thought you told me there was no occult activity in your history?" With a much more humble attitude, fighting through the crying, she assured me she hadn't done anything like that. "Then why did I just hear the word witchcraft?" I said.

This poor woman was a mess, at this point. First, we are going on five hours of this. Second, she's on an emotional rollercoaster, having had so many ailments, then so much deliverance, followed by this obvious demonic attack on the level of the film, The Exorcist. With her spirit completely broken, she sobbed and said, "I assure you, I've done nothing." Just then, I saw an image, a brief picture of an older woman with gray hair and I relayed that to her. I told her, "Whoever it is, they brought witchcraft into your home, and I think it's your mother." Just then she yelled out, "My mother, she bought us a ouija board when I was five." I yelled at her, "Get on your knees and repent woman." I'm just saying... you had to be there. I heard her knees hit the floor and she said, "Father, in the name of Jesus, forgive me." Just then, she let out a screech, but it was different than the others, it was like a sigh of relief and she said, "It's gone, it just left, I felt it go."

The first way you give up Authority is by doing nothing, and the second way you give up your Authority is sin. Just as Adam's sin gave his Authority away in the garden, our sin hands our Authority away, as well. Participating in any form of occult activity, no matter how innocuous it seems, is sin. The two main ways we give up our Authority through sin is occult activity and sexual immorality, or sex outside of marriage. These are not the only two, but they are the main two and upon this behavior, Authority is given to a spirit that enters you. Once that spirit gains entry, it has the legal right to stay until Authority is taken away. People who say that a spirit cannot enter a Christian, have no clue what they are talking about. They can, and do, all the time. I know this, because it happened to me.

> *You are to consult neither mediums nor familiar spirits.*
> *You are never to seek them, you'll just be defiled by*
> *them. I am the LORD your God.* Leviticus 19:31

> *But the man who was healed did not know who healed*
> *him... Afterward, Jesus found the man at the temple*
> *and said to him, "See, you have been made well. Stop*
> *sinning, or something worse may happen to you."*
> John 5:13-14

I would soon learn that sin, in the form of occult activity, causes mental and emotional issues, but they, also, usher in other spirits that bring affliction and disease. Sexual sin caused most, if not all of the physical ailments that afflicted the cases that I've done. The occult activity opens the door to demonic spirits that afflict the mind in the form of extreme sadness, depression, schizophrenia, suicide, anger, rage, and even murder. In order to evict the demonic spirits, Authority must be taken back and this is where repentance and forgiveness come in.

Some sickness and disease come by way of occult activity. I know this, because of the cases I've done where the people had dabbled in the occult, but had not committed sexual sin, yet still had many physical ailments, as well as, many mental problems. Sexual sin on the other hand, is sin against your own body, and affected my case subjects with severe physical ailments only. This is confirmed by Paul in 1 Corinthians,

Flee from sexual immorality. Every other sin a man can commit is outside his body, but he who sins sexually sins against his own body. 1 Corinthians 6:18

Sinning against your own body is equivalent to deliberately injuring yourself. I know there are spirits that self-mutilate, but most people would not willingly inflict serious, long-lasting harm to themselves, yet, that is exactly what sexual sin does. As with occult activity, sexual sin hands over your Authority to the demonic spirit to enter you and causes a number of sicknesses and diseases, as well as, physical ailments. I found it interesting that many of my case subjects were sexually active in their younger years, during college and such, but had not been so for 20 or 30 years. It was only after all that time that the symptoms began to present themselves. This implies that the spirit lay dormant for all those years before it manifested itself, making it nearly impossible to associate with the behavior, because of the span of time between the two. Had it not been for the Holy Spirit telling me what to do and how to do it, I see no way to have been able to connect the sin to the ailment.

Why is it that nobody is teaching about Authority? Why is the church only focused on prosperity? Because prosperity is being used as a distraction from the four most important lessons a believer needs to know after salvation, Identity, Authority, Power of Words, and Love. With The Altar of Love, God showed me the lessons to teach and the order in which to teach them, so that a believer could walk, talk, and portray themselves just like Jesus. First, they must understand who they are in Christ Jesus, they must know their Identity. Second, they must know what Authority is and how to utilize it. Third, they must master their Words. Lastly, they must walk in Love.

So what happened? How is it that these important lessons have not only been neglected, but more than that, one could say that they have been hidden from the body of Christ. The Devil is no fool. As soon as, He realized that He had lost Authority, He immediately regrouped to develop a plan to get it back. Maybe He huddled up his closest demons and requested suggestions and ideas of what to do now that Authority was lost. Maybe a demon suggested that they could infiltrate the churches, corrupt the teachers and hide the Identity and Authority of a believer by distracting them with cares of the world, deceitfulness of riches, and the desire for other things, as in the Parable of the Sower. Maybe another demon suggested that once the church is distracted from teaching Identity and Authority, they could then steal Authority away from the believer. You see, Authority is there for the taking. If we don't assume it, Satan will.

Picture it like this, every believer has had a demon posted by them since you were born. One of their jobs is to observe you and report back to Satan. They mess with you, sowing lies and deceptions and watch your reactions. Do you get angry easily? Do you get sad or depressed? Are you negative or hard on yourself? Are you prone to gossip or backbiting? Are you selfish, greedy, or envious of what others have? They observe all of these things, so they can use them against you. Are you easily addicted to drugs or alcohol? Or is it money, sex, or power that motivates you? Whatever it is, they set traps to make you fall into sin for the sole purpose of taking your Authority. This transfer of Authority gives them the legal right to wreak havoc in your life, or the lives of those associated to you.

After the cross, the demons were given another more important job, looking for opportunities to take your Authority. They know how valuable and powerful it is, and they certainly do not want you using it against them. There are five ways they can take your Authority, and the first one is when a believer does nothing. As I said before, Authority is there for the taking, but if we do not assume it, they will. Picture a demon standing next to you, arms folded and he's tapping his fingers on his bicep, saying, "What are you going to do here? Authority is available in this situation. Are you going to assume it? Because if you don't, I will."

Most Christians do not even know that they have Authority. Some Christians know about Authority, but they have no real understanding of what it is. A few know what Authority is, but will not assume it. The most frustrating group are the ones that think, by leaving Satan alone, He will leave them alone. Nothing could be farther from the truth. He is an equal opportunity destroyer, and like all bullies, they prey on the weak and helpless. The only thing they respect, the only thing that keeps them in check or at bay is an adopted child of the Most High God exercising Authority.

Another one of Satan's deceptions are the believers that have been duped into thinking that they are not supposed to engage the enemy, incorrectly quoting this verse in Jude,

But Michael the archangel, when he disputed with the Devil and argued about the body of Moses, did not dare pronounce against him a railing judgment, but said, The Lord rebuke you! Jude 1:9

Sounds correct, right? No, we are not the angels, we are children and we have different responsibilities than angels.

The Word says that the angels hearken unto the Word of God, but Jesus said we were given Authority. The angels' job is to do the Word of God, to carry it out. They work for God, not us, but we are the ones here sowing the Word. Therefore, one of their jobs is to perform the Word that we speak or sow. In Mark 4 (the Parable of the Sower), Jesus illustrates the Kingdom of God, as a man who scatters seed. We are that farmer and the seed is the Word of God, that we sow in the form of prayer or Authority. Binding and loosing come into play here, as well. When we bind the works, powers and plans of the enemy, we are not the ones holding the Devil accountable, the angels are. They facilitate, that which, we bind or loose.

> *Bless the LORD, O you his angels, you mighty ones who do his word, obeying the voice of his word!* Psalm 130:20

Whether we are praying, binding, loosing or assuming authority, it's the job of the angels to make it happen. Each person has two Angels assigned to them for the sole purpose of ministering to us, guiding us, protecting us, facilitating the answer to our prayers and assuming the Authority we take. That is, providing we are within our legal right, our Authority, to do so. If, out of arrogance, we attempt to assume Authority over something we have no authority over, then our angels are under no obligation to perform that task.

In order for us to operate successfully in the Kingdom of God, we must line up with and according to the Word and/or the Will of God. Unlike angels, we are Children of God, co-heirs to the throne with Authority over all the power of the enemy. Therefore, you cannot compare our role to that of the angels. We have different jobs, as we have different positions in the Kingdom. We are children and they are servants.

An accurate analogy would be comparing the difference between a child and an employee of a business owner. The owner may love his employees, but they are still just employees. No matter how loyal and faithful they may be, they will never take the place of the child. Even if the kids are not well-behaved, they are still the ones that receive the inheritance. If an employee messes up, repentance or not, he's fired. However, if a child messes up, and asks forgiveness, he's forgiven, no matter how many times it happens. It's a totally different relationship. In the book of Enoch, many of the fallen angels had regretted what they had done and sent a letter to God by way of Enoch asking for forgiveness, but God said no, absolutely not.

There are some things not under our Authority, so it is important for us to understand what things we have Authority over and what things we do not. Where does Authority end and prayer begin? There were times when Jesus prayed about things and there were times He took Authority and just spoke to them. As we already learned, He said we had Authority over Satan and all demon powers and over all diseases. That's easy enough, if it's demonic or illness, it's under our Authority. But what about people? Do I have Authority over people? No and yes! Because God made us with a free will, I have no Authority over another person, unless they are under my Authority as children, or unless they give their Authority to me.

A person can acquiesce their Authority to another if they ask that person to pray for them. If they allow me, I can take Authority over any demonic spirits that are afflicting them, but if they refuse, if I ask them to pray for them and they say no, I have no Authority to bind the spirits and cast them off. In areas not under our Authority, your only recourse is prayer.

Now prayer is powerful, but it is not more powerful than one's free will. Usually, if a person refuses prayer, it's because that spirit has such a hold over them that they do not want it removed. They have grown quite fond of the spirit, they like the behavior they are engaging in, and do not want to stop. You cannot make someone want to be free from the yoke of sin, if they are enjoying the sin they are engaging in. Jesus gives us a brilliant explanation of the difference between Authority and prayer in Mark 11,

Truly, I say to you, whoever says to this mountain, Be taken up and thrown into the sea, and does not doubt in his heart, but believes that what he says will come to pass, it will be done for him. Therefore I tell you, whatever you ask in prayer, believe that you have received it, and it will be yours. Mark 11:23 & 24

Verse 23 indicates Authority, but verse 24 indicates prayer. In 23, He is simply directing us to speak to the thing under our Authority. He's not instructing us to ask God to do it, He's telling us to assume Authority with our words, and as long as we know our Identity, as long as we know our Authority and as long as we believe what we've taken Authority over must obey us, we will have whatever we say. In verse 24, Jesus is describing how prayer works. He says, whatever we pray for, if we believe we, will receive and we will have it.

Regarding both prayer and Authority, it is imperative that we consider what God's Will is regarding the circumstance. This may seem like an impossible task, but I assure you, it is easier than you think. God's Will is His Word. If you read and study his Word, you will know His Will. Occasionally, you will face a situation that is out of your realm of expertise or knowledge. When that happens and you do not know what to do, because you don't know what God's Will is for it, that's a perfect time to pray for wisdom.

> *If any of you lacks wisdom, let him ask God, who gives generously to all without reproach, and it will be given him.* James 1:5

Chapter Five

The Power of Our Words: Leg 3, Part 1 of The Altar of Love

Death and life are in the power of the tongue and those who love it will eat its fruit. Proverbs 18:21

Many years ago, Pastor, Jim Scalise made the most interesting comment that proceeded to change the direction of my spiritual walk forever. "When the Devil was cast out of Heaven he was stripped of his spiritual power," he said. I do not remember anything else pertaining to that sermon, because for some unknown reason, I could not get that statement out of my mind.

It is obvious that the Devil has power, just a quick look at the world around us, and the aftermath of his destructive nature is clearly evident. Murder, violence, drugs and alcoholism, corporate theft of billions of hard earned retirements, wars, rampant homosexuality, mega storms, crimes against women and children, terrorism, you name it and it's happening everywhere. Many of the present crimes against humanity make the behavior of Sodom and Gomorrah look like an episode of Leave it to Beaver. Oh no, the Devil has power, that much I knew. But if the Devil was stripped of his spiritual power, what power does he have?

All the way home I could think of nothing else. As the hours passed I drifted back to life as usual. That evening, however, lying awake for hours in bed, I pondered the question... what power does the Devil really have? After many hours, I finally fell asleep only to awake to the same question racing through my mind. As was my habit, I made some coffee and sat in my living room with my Bible attempting to continue a study I had been working on involving Genesis 6 and the Giants, in those days.

The once exciting study seemed to come to an abrupt end that day, as all my attention surrounded my new ten million dollar question, what power does the Devil really have? I put my Bible down and began to pray, "Heavenly Father, your word says in James 1, if any man lacks wisdom, let him ask and it shall be given to him liberally and without reproach. Therefore, Father, in the name of the Lord Jesus, I ask for wisdom regarding this question, which confounds me. If the Devil was stripped of his spiritual power, what power does he have? Wisdom come in the name of Jesus. I thank you Father for your word that never returns to you void, but always accomplishes what it was sent to do, in Jesus name, Amen."

Each day my appetite for the answer to this question only increased as I studied my Bible looking for a word, a verse, anything that God might use to show me what I was looking for. As often as I thought of it, I reminded God of his promise to give wisdom to anyone who asks.

So I say to you, ask and it will be given to you; seek and you shall find; knock and it will be opened to you. For everyone who asks receives, and he who seeks finds, and to him who knocks it will be opened. If a son asks for bread from any father among you, will he give him a stone? Or if he asks for a fish will he give him a serpent instead of a fish? Or if he asks for an egg, will he offer him a scorpion? If you then, being evil, know how to give good gifts to your children, how much more will your Heavenly Father give the Holy Spirit to those who ask him? Luke 11:9

Don't get me wrong, I was not asking in unbelief. That is when you ask, "Oh God, please provide this need for me, in Jesus name." Then the following day when the answer has not arrived you do it again, "Oh God, please provide this need for me, in Jesus name." I found the scripture that pertained to my situation, I confessed it in prayer and thanked God for it even though it had not yet come to pass. The following day when it had not been made manifest in the natural, I simply reminded God of his word. "Father, your Word says it would not return to You void, but must accomplish what you please."

Be like the Jewish woman who kept going back to the Judge when he finally just gave up and granted her request. The only difference is that judge was not God and in his unrighteousness she had to keep asking him for relief to her problem. It's a little different for us, in that, we simply need to remind God of his word or the promise that He made to us in His Word.

One day, I received a call from Pastor Jim Scalise concerning a member of the church and a martial arts student that I put in business as a type of franchise several years earlier. During our conversation Pastor Scalise indicated that the Lord had just revealed to him during prayer that this man was under serious attack from the Evil One, and that I should contact him and restore him.

I promptly called the gentleman and tried to arrange a meeting, but he stonewalled me. Every time I suggested a time of meeting, he squashed it, but one time he hesitated, so I confirmed it and got off the phone before he could change his mind. When I got to his business, he was not there, but as I was leaving the parking lot I saw him in his truck attempting a quick getaway. I pulled alongside him and urged him to park his car at his office.

I drove him to a nearby restaurant, asked him what was wrong and immediately he began to weep. He sobbed like a child for several minutes before he could compose himself enough to speak. He told me how he felt immense pressure at work and at home. His wife was spending their money faster than the business could make it, he battled daily with his stepchildren, the business had become stressful and laborious, and he felt like he was losing his mind. He, also, said that he was thinking about leaving my business organization. As he spoke these things to me, God showed me in the spirit that he was battling with a spirit of depression.

I ministered the word to him reminding him of the promises of God and encouraging him to take a strong stand in the face of trials. I felt the Lord prompt me to share James 1:1-3 with him. *My brethren, count it all joy when you fall into various trials, knowing that the testing of your faith produces patience.* Now that word 'patience,' I said, is more accurately translated, consistency. When trials come, I explained, you have two choices, you can react the way the world does or you can do what the Word says. If you do what Jesus did, praying about it and trusting God or taking Authority over it, you will see miraculous results.

The next time a trial arises, I said, if you are wise you will remember how the Lord delivered you from your past tribulation and you will do it God's way again. Now, every time you are confronted with a new trial you can have joy in the midst of that trial knowing that your consistent nature, which automatically prompts you to pray and take Authority, will produce miraculous results.

Wallowing in self-pity, but desperate to try anything to relieve the torment he was under, he reluctantly submitted to the Word. As I drove him back to his office, I placed my hand upon his shoulder and began to pray over him. Upon completion, he opened the door and stepped out of the car; leaning in through the window he reached out his hand to shake mine. I could see on his face that his countenance had completely changed, as he was smiling from ear to ear. He thanked me enthusiastically and bounded into his business. Speaking with him the following day, he explained that evening was the best he had ever felt.

As I drove away, I immediately felt deep despair. I began to think of the remarks he had made about leaving my martial arts organization. Instead of focusing upon the positive results of the meeting, I could think of nothing other than the fact that he was even considering leaving. How could he do that to me? I thought. I taught him everything he knows, I put him in business, and I signed the lease on his behalf assuming full responsibility if he failed, a financial sum exceeding $300,000. After he was turned down for his business loan, I convinced my banker to give him the loan upon my word, that it would be repaid.

I sat in his business for weeks preregistering customers, so that he could continue working at his other job. And because I located him so close to me, I even sent 40% of my customers to his location, so that he would start with an existing clientele base, enabling him to open his doors with a profit from day one. After all I had done for him, how he dare even entertain the idea of stealing this business from me.

Horrible thoughts raced through my mind. My anger grew with every minute that passed. Thoughts of despair, thoughts of anger, and finally, thoughts of depression appeared, as I began to think that this successful organization that I had built over the last two decades, might be falling apart. I arrived back at my martial arts center just in time to teach my 5 pm class, when I felt the Holy Spirit say, **Pray.** Realizing I was dealing with the same spirit that had plagued him, I noticed the clock indicated it was time for class to begin, so I figured I would pray after class. This was a big mistake.

For twenty years I had taught class with passion and enthusiasm. In all those years, I have no memory of ever watching the clock waiting for classes to end. On the contrary, I was usually hard pressed to cover all the material I desired to teach and ended every class wishing I had more time, but not this day. Every class seamed to drag on forever as depressing thoughts filled my head, and I knew that prayer was the only thing I needed. I was a miserable and useless instructor that day.

Finally, my last class ended, so I went to my office to pray, and just then, my phone rang. One of my closest friends was inviting me to meet them for dinner, but to hurry, because they were already there. I know I should have prayed right then and there, but I putting it off for some reason. I called my wife to ask permission to go, because a married man who leaves his wife at home with two children to go off to dinner at one of her favorite restaurants, without permission deserves all the trouble he gets. As I drove to the restaurant, I felt the Holy Spirit prompt me to pray, but I just kept putting it off.

As I walked in the restaurant, my friend was on his cell phone, raising one hand in a gesture of 'hello,' then he went back to his call. I sat down across from his wife, and looking up at me she pushed herself away from the table and said. "What is all over you?" Surprised that she could see it, I proceeded to tell her the day's events. Once again, instead of praying over my problem we talked about it, allowing me to wallow further in this quagmire of depression. Romans 8:31 says, *What then shall we say to these things?*

I have since learned the importance of Romans 8:31. Not What shall we say about these things? but, *What shall we say to these things?* Instead of talking about our problems, Christians are instructed to take Authority over them by speaking to their problems. Jesus confirmed this in Mark 11:23 when he said, *For assuredly, I say to you, whoever says to this mountain, 'Be removed and be cast into the sea,' and does not doubt in his heart, but believes that those things he says will be done, he will have whatever he says.* Our problems, our circumstances, our issues in this life are the mountains that Jesus was talking about, and He is demonstrating how we should deal with that problem, by talking **to** it, not about it. When I talk about my problem, I am only feeding it by giving it my Authority and making it stronger.

So, the big question is, **what** shall we say to these things? Or, what do we say to our problems? What did Jesus do when He had a problem? Every time Satan tempted Jesus in the desert, Jesus responded with the Word of God that directly countered the Devil's attack. When we have a problem, like Jesus, we must quote the scripture that directly pertains to the problem. Then we stand, in faith, until our answer is manifest, regardless of how long it takes.

The problem for many people is that they cannot quote something they do not know. Mat. 12:34 says, ***Out of the abundance of the heart the mouth speaks.*** Everything that we experience goes into our heart. Everything we witness, everything we watch, everything we listen to, all of it goes into our heart and out of the abundance of our heart, the mouth speaks.

When people say foolish things, hurtful things, evil things, deceitful things it is because that is what they have been putting into their heart. That is the very reason new, well-intentioned Christians will say foolish or insensitive things, because for their entire lives they have been putting worldly junk into their heart and that is the only thing that can come out. Eventually, as they renew their minds with the Word, it will happen less and less often, until it happens no more. One must continually remind oneself to be patient with new believers and not let their remarks offend them.

> ***For where your treasure is there your heart will be also.***
> Matt 6:21

> ***A good man out of the good treasure of his heart brings forth good things, and an evil man out of the evil treasure brings forth evil.*** Matt 12:35

So, we see here that a person's heart is referred to as their treasure. How are we treating the treasure that is our heart? When I think of a treasure, I think of a chest filled with precious gems like diamonds, rubies, and emeralds. I picture it

106

overflowing with gold coins and gold jewelry, so valuable that one could not put a price tag upon it. If you had a treasure like this, how would you treat it? Would you just leave it out in the back yard where the sun would fade it's brilliance and the rain, dust, dirt would tarnish it? Would you use it as a toilet in your house? Absolutely not! You would place it in the safest place of the house and you would give it the utmost care. That is the way we should care for our heart, letting nothing enter it that may corrupt it, because out of our heart, out of our treasure, we speak.

When you have a problem, don't talk about it, but rather take Authority over it and command it to line up with the Will of God. If someone you know comes to you with a problem, don't allow yourself to be dragged into a discussion about it, simply ask them if they would like to pray about it and **let it go**! Many times I have prayed for people and immediately after prayer they would start talking about their problem again. This can be very tricky since you do not want to seem insensitive. However, you have to be careful that you do not nullify everything you just prayed for by talking about or feeding the mountain you are trying to move. Also, remember that, when someone has a problem and you pray for them, it blesses them and you, as well.

> *Do not be deceived, God will not be mocked, for whatever a man sows, that shall he also reap.* Gal 6:7

If this is true, and we know it is, because God said it, then when you pray for others you are sowing seeds for yourself, and there may come a day when someone will pray for you when you need it most.

With that foul spirit still attached to me, I was driving home from the dinner and, I remember saying to myself, I should pray. By this time, however, the will to do so was no longer there, because we spent so much time talking about my problem instead of taking Authority over it. Arriving at home around midnight, I knew my wife would be in bed. My wife was such a sound sleeper, that it made me jealous. I could get in and out of bed, turn on the TV, and even make or receive a phone call, and most of the time she wouldn't even stir.

This day, however, was different. As soon as, I entered the dark bedroom, she sat up and turned the light on so fast it startled me. How did she do that? I thought, I was as quiet as a mouse. She looked around the room, then directly at me and said, "What is on you and why have you brought it into my house?" Before I could go into the dramatic story, again, she interrupted me and said, "Come over here and pray first."

Finally, I thought, but then this thing came over me and as I heard the words coming out of my mouth, to this day, I still cannot believe I said them, "I don't want to," I replied. I tried to get back to my pitiful story, when she interrupted me, again, and said, "Lets pray." I knew in my heart that that was exactly what I needed, but my head was telling me otherwise. "I don't want to," I said, again. "Francis Santarose," she said, "in the name of Jesus you get over here right now and pray with me." At that name, I was powerless not to, so reluctantly, I agreed, and as soon as she laid her hand on my arm and said, "In the name of Jesus," I felt the spirit of depression leave and peace came flowing over me.

What God showed me later through that episode was to pray immediately, because every moment I allowed the spirit to stay made its hold over me harder to resist. I, also, learned not to look down upon people who are dealing with demonic strongholds like depression, anger, jealousy, unforgiveness, and such, because even mature Christians can be deceived.

Think of it like this, everything either comes from God or the Devil. There is nothing else. There is no third point of view. This is not Star Trek, and there is no Neutral Zone. There is only God's way of thinking and doing things, or there is the Devil's way. In the Bible, the Devil's way is referred to as the way of the world. If you want to know what the way of the world is, just observe pop culture. Spend a day watching cable TV, see the sex, the violence, the decadence, listen to the anger, hatred, vulgarity, and lust. I say that for those of you that do not have cable TV, like me.

Having been on vacation with my family, one sleepless night, I scanned the cable channels in our hotel room. The things that bombarded my conscious mind through the visuals that passed before my eyes were appalling. These poor kids and what they have to deal with. It's unfair. How is a pre-teen/teenager supposed to make good decisions when everything they see and hear cries sin? Satan has successfully captured the airways, and fills our children with his vulgar and disgusting way of thinking, on a daily basis. Only a fool would refuse to admit that Sodom and Gomorrah have nothing on this present generation.

Remember my initial question of what power does the Devil have? That was Sunday, and only three days after I began praying for wisdom, I got my answer. If the Devil was stripped of his spiritual power, what power does he have? On Wednesday night, I went to sleep as usual, but I awoke at 4 am.

I felt wide awake, but I tried to go back to sleep, so I grabbed my pillow, rolled over to my most comfortable sleeping position, and relaxed. Suddenly, my eyes bugged wide open. I rolled over the other way, but soon realized that I was not going back to sleep, so I might as well get up and pray. I could feel a strong sense of urgency, not danger, just importance. This was definitely different from anything I'd felt before.

Moving to the living room, I knelt down, lifted my hands and began to pray. I prayed about everything that my mind could think of, when suddenly I felt something urge me to stop talking. This was not a voice, but an urge or unction. It was compelling me to be quiet. It was as if the Holy Spirit was telling me to hush-up, but it wasn't rude. It happened telepathically, and it was really sweet. Basically, I understood that I was to stop talking, because the Lord wanted to talk and if we were going to have a conversation, I needed to learn how to be quiet long enough for Him to tell me something.

I sat back on my heals for a few seconds when suddenly, a very loud, thundering voice from above me began to speak. ***The power that the Devil has is the power that you give him by the words that you speak.*** I knelt there in amazement, as I tried to grasp what just happened. The power that the Devil has is the power that I give him by the words that I speak! WOW, that is huge, I thought. Oh my goodness, the enormity of it began to sink in. Suddenly, I wondered who else heard it, because it was that loud. I jumped up and ran to my bedroom to see if Angela heard it, as well. She was sound asleep, but that was not unusual as she could sleep through almost anything. I went to Francisco's room, because he is a light sleeper like me, but he was asleep, too. I didn't even bother with Joseph, because he sleeps like a log.

Too excited and desperately needing to share what was just entrusted to me, I called my brother. As soon as I heard his voice, I blurted it out, "The power that the Devil has is the power that we give him by the words that we speak." "Huh?" he responded. Speaking 100 miles an hour and hardly able to contain myself, I said it again and I gave him the briefest explanation of what just happened, including the events that led to it. "Wow," was pretty much all he could muster, followed by a long pause and finally he said, "That explains a lot of things, yea, that makes a whole lot of sense." "Do you realize what this means?" I asked. "Not entirely, because it's late, but we certainly need to discuss it some more. Call me tomorrow."

After I hung up the phone I went to the kitchen to make some coffee, because there was just no way I was going back to sleep now. I stood there and began to meditate upon the Rhema Word that was spoken to me. That's when I could hear the Holy Spirit speaking to me down in my spirit in this soft voice telling me in great detail the meaning of it all. He said, *The same power that I used to create the heavens and the earth when I spoke them into existence, I placed within man. But throughout time, man has misused this great power with the misuse of his words. Satan, understanding the power within words, and having been stripped of that power simply steels it from man by manipulating him into speaking what he (Satan) wills for man. Remember that Satan comes only to kill, steal and destroy, therefore, watch with all diligence every word that you speak and by doing so, you will give no place, no power, and no Authority to the Devil.*

Just then, I saw a vision of Abraham, Lot, and seven herdsman sitting around a campfire. Lot had a stick that he used to poke the fire occasionally. In the spirit realm, there is no time, so while the vision only lasted a few minutes, I knew that 5 or 6 hours had transpired and nobody said a word. Then I heard a voice say, *The ancients understood the power of their words and only spoke when necessary, likewise, be a man of few words.*

That's when I remembered Proverbs 18:21, *Death and life are in the power of the tongue,* and as I contemplated why it said death first, I heard, *Death first, because man is more likely to speak death than life over their situation.* When my wife awoke, I told her all that happened and together we prayed for confirmation. The following Sunday, as we sat waiting for service to begin, our pastor said a dear friend of his had called him with a remarkable vision she had while coming home from a mission trip in Africa. Her name was Ralphina Dodson, and he turned the service over to her to share her vision.

She was tall, impeccably dressed, and had a remarkably strong presence. As she began to speak, it was obvious she was anointed to preach the gospel, but I would soon learn that she was much more than that. She began by telling us about her trip home from Africa. As she was sitting in her seat, she felt herself being lifted out of her body looking down at herself and she realized she was in the spirit. What she would see next would forever change her life, as she passionately described this vision from God.

She saw an old time ice cube tray, the metal kind, which were used before the plastic ones trays were produced. For those under 40, ice cube trays were made of metal with a metal bar on top that you pulled upward to crack and release the cubes. It was inferior to the present day trays, however, it was functional. As she looked at the tray she said, "Lord, what does it mean?" *Look closer*, The Lord replied. As she looked closer she saw the metal bar lift up and pull out releasing the cubes. Once again she said, "Lord, what does it mean?" *Look closer*, He replied.

As she looked closer the tray turned upside down and the tray itself lifted off, but the cubes remained stuck together. Once again she said, "Lord, what does it mean?" *Look closer*, He replied. Suddenly she noticed the cubes were over the Earth, specifically over the United States. As she looked closer, she noticed there was a glue-like substance holding the cubes together. Once again she asked God what it was and once again He told her to look closer. As she looked closer, she noticed the glue holding the cubes together were words, and the cubes themselves represented the power or stronghold that Satan has over the earth.

She saw words of negativity, vulgarity, despair, unbelief; every evil thing that came out of the mouth of man since the flood of Noah was going up into the atmosphere and being used by the Devil to strengthen his hold over the world. Suddenly, she looked up and in a loud, authoritative voice she said, "The power that the Devil has is the power that we give him by the words that we speak." Word for word, this is what was spoken to me. Angela and I just looked at each other in amazement, each of us with goose bumps on top of our goose bumps. I met Miss Ralphena after the service and told her what I experienced the week before. She gave me her number and asked to meet me, so that we could discuss it further. We have been very close friends ever since.

> **Behold, I have seen a son of Jesse the Bethlehemite, that is cunning in playing, and a mighty valiant man, and a man of war, and prudent in matters.** 1 Sam 16:18

'Prudent' is translated from the word 'bin,' which is defined as, 'to consider carefully.' 'Matters' is translated from the word 'Dabar' and it means, words. So David, from his youth was reputed to carefully consider his words before he spoke. David knew how dangerous words were and how to use them wisely.

As the third leg of The Altar of Love, The Power of Words is actually two parts. First, it is the Power of the Words that we speak about our situation, either negatively or positively.

Remember, there are five ways you give up your Authority. The first way is by doing nothing. Authority is there for the assuming. If we don't, Satan will. The second way is by sin and the third way is with our words. When you say something negative about your situation, something contrary to what God says, you are handing over your Authority and Satan will gladly use it against you.

Have you ever had an old song go through your mind all day, because you heard it briefly on the radio? All the words and the melody come flooding back, and no matter how hard you try, you just can't stop replaying that song in your mind. That does not even come close to the suggestive power the enemy has over us. While that song may replay in our minds, because we heard it one time, Satan has a demon stationed near you to repeat a lie over and over and over. As well, he will likely usher in several other demon friends who specialize in similar fields of suggestion and persuasion with the intent to break down your will power.

All of this, all this effort, all this time is devoted to one cause... to get you to say IT. He needs you to say IT! Say what? Say IT! What is IT? IT is the very thing he is trying to get you to say, so that He can take your Authority and use IT against you. "I have cancer, You're a loser, I'm stupid, I hate you, I hate myself, You'll never amount to anything," etc. If it's mean, hurtful, negative, or condemning, he's trying to get you to say it, because when you do, he's got your Authority. Remember, the power the Devil has is the power we give him by the words that we speak. The power God is referring to here is our Authority, our Superpower. Satan can take away our Superpower, by hijacking our words.

The weapons of our warfare are not carnal but mighty in God for pulling down strongholds, casting down arguments and every high thing that exalts itself against the knowledge of God, bringing every thought into captivity to the obedience of Christ. 2 Cor. 10:4-6

Paul says it perfectly here. Your fight is not with your boss, or your neighbor, or your co-worker, or even your spouse. Just like you, they are under bombardment with suggestions to lie, cheat, steal, cuss, and fornicate; you name it, and they're going through it. God is instructing us in how to handle this assault by telling us to take every thought into captivity and hold it to the standard, which is the Word, to see where it comes from. But how many people, even mature Christians, do you think have the sense to do just that? The number is much smaller that you can imagine.

First of all, most believers would never even think of doing this. They've been in church for years and the only thing they know about is prosperity. Second, the ones that have read and learned of this verse, never consider actually putting it into practice. The third and final group just don't put it into practice, but not because they don't know how. More likely than not, it is because they are tired. They've been fighting the good fight of faith for decades, but the enemy has worn them down. It is a most difficult task to do alone, we need each other.

We are instructed to take **every** thought into captivity to the obedience of Christ. Every thought! Hello, every thought! How many thoughts do you think we have in a day? 10,000? 30,000? 50,000? I really don't know, but the mere thought of that alone is exhausting. Maybe that's what Paul meant when he said, "Do not grow weary of doing good."

God has placed within us the power of the spoken Word, the same power He used to create the Earth, but mankind has misused this power since the days of old. Every negative ugly comment, every cuss word, everything that comes out of a man's mouth that does not edify another, is used by the enemy.

> *Let no corrupt word proceed out of your mouth, but what is good for necessary edification, that it may impart grace to the hearers.* Eph 4:29

Satan has nothing, no power over us what-so-ever, except that which we give him by the words that we speak. However, He brilliantly figured out how to get us to speak against ourselves and hand over our Authority to Him in the process. Remember,

He has been around for 6,000 years, that we know of, but He may have fallen a million years ago. There is just no record of time before the creation of the world, and since Satan was in the garden with Adam and Eve, he certainly has a lot of experience with this. His main weapon is the power of suggestion. For most people in the world, and carnal Christians, as well, he suggests it, and because there is very little to no self-control these days, they either repeat it, or do it.

For people with more discipline, who aren't just going to say every word or perform every foolish act that pops in their head, Satan has a more subtle, yet just as destructive, approach. He knows the scripture. As Lucifer, he used to use the power of the spoken word before it was stripped from Him.

How you are fallen from Heaven, O Lucifer, son of the morning! How you are cut down to the ground, You who weakened the nations! For you have said in your heart: I will ascend into Heaven, I will exalt my throne above the stars of God; I will also sit on the mount of the congregation, On the farthest sides of the north; I will ascend above the heights of the clouds, I will be like the Most High. Isaiah 14:12

Here we clearly see Satan trying to use the power of his words to accomplish His overthrow of God, but God will not be outspoken and had the last word when He said, *Yet you shall be brought down to Sheol, To the lowest depths of the Pit. Those who see you will gaze at you, And consider you, saying: Is this the man who made the earth tremble, Who shook kingdoms, Who made the world as a wilderness, And destroyed its cities, But you are cast out of your grave, Like an abominable branch, Like the garment of those who are slain,*

__Thrust through with a sword, Who go down to the stones of the pit, Like a corpse trodden underfoot. You will not be joined with them in burial.__ Isaiah 14:15-20

For more disciplined believers, people who will not just bite on every lure that Satan casts before them. He simply uses their own words against them. He gets them to say what He wants them to say, just by suggesting it to them. Contrary to conventional wisdom, this is as true for believers as unbelievers. Knowing this, you'd think that believers would be much better than unbelievers at watching their words, but you'd be surprised. Some days, I think that unbelievers are better at watching their words than Christians. Probably because Satan has assigned his most cunning demons to destroy believers. The days of being appalled when mature Christians fall, are long since passed, it's now commonplace.

It doesn't take a rocket scientist to understand that believers are not perfect, just saved. Many believers came to salvation, because they totally messed up and they had nowhere else to turn, but up. They are flawed people, people with a past, an imperfect people who humbled themselves before the mighty Hand of God. Believers do not automatically become perfect when they get saved. For years, they will make many of the same old mistakes as they walk out their salvation, leaving many casualties in their wake. But if they do not lose heart, if they continue to submit to Bible-based teaching, and if they confess their sins and repent, they will grow and a renewing of the mind will begin to change them from the inside out. They begin to look less like the world and more like their King Jesus.

As well, they have a new enemy that does not want them to know their Identity or their Authority. Satan cannot afford for them to learn that they are adopted children of the most-high God, joint-heirs with Christ who come boldly before the Throne of God, where they can obtain grace and mercy in their time of need.

For if they ever figure out that they have Authority over all the power of the enemy, as Jesus said, the enemy is a defeated foe. So, he mounts a relentless attack when they are young in the Lord and as we learned earlier, if they will not simply act upon his suggestion, he will regroup and try to get them to say their destruction. Either way, he is bent upon destruction.

Using ones words against oneself takes a little longer and requires a more cunning, experienced demon, but the results will eventually be the same. He suggests it, we repeat it, and He reaps the fruit of the thing we just spoke. He knows that whatever we speak with our mouth and believe in our heart will come to pass.

For assuredly, I say to you, whoever says to this mountain, 'Be removed and be cast into the sea,' and does not doubt in his heart, but believes that those things he says will be done, he will have whatever he says. Mark 11:23

Now, Jesus never spoke just to hear himself speak, and as I said before, He never, ever, came back to his disciples and said, "Ya know, that thing about speaking to mountains, that didn't come out quite right." No, He knew that every time He opened His mouth to speak, it was exactly what our God wanted us to know, and at the exact time He wanted us to know it.

Furthermore, every time Jesus begins a teaching by saying, *Verily, verily I say unto thee,* or *Assuredly I say,* we had better take an extra long look and try to understand exactly what He is saying. It's like He is holding up a megaphone saying, "HEY, STOP WHAT YOUR DOING, LOOK THIS WAY AND PAY ATTENTION, BECAUSE THE NEXT THING I HAVE TO SAY IS REALLY IMPORTANT!" That is the meaning of, Assuredly I say!

As well, Jesus is not speaking to believers only, as many assume, and that is proven by the word, "whoever." Reread it and notice the word, "whoever." A study on the Greek word for "whoever" means, anyone, period. Mark 11:23 is an enormously powerful verse as Jesus is trying to get his followers to understand the power of their words. This is a spiritual law, and this particular spiritual law works in every direction, with believers or unbelievers, good or bad, for or against you, all depending upon what words come out of your mouth.

As well, Satan is constantly working some scheme and He knows just how to get us to say that thing He will use against us. On the flip side, Our Father loves us and He has given us weapons to overcome the Evil One. First, He gave us His Word. If we will read His Word it will go into us. If it goes into us long enough, it will eventually come out, and when it comes out it defeats the Evil One, every time, all the time. He, also, gave us the ultimate superpower, Authority, and with Authority, nothing can harm us and nothing is impossible for us. But again, it comes down to our words. The power the Devil has is the power we give Him by the words that we speak.

Here's a challenge... take one week and notice everything that comes out of your mouth. By notice, I mean notice whether your words are positive or negative, nice or mean, helpful or hurtful. Then, the next week, let nothing come out of your mouth that does not line up with what Jesus said or would say.

If you have ever taken the time to really read the Gospels, Mathew, Mark, Luke, and John, you will notice that Jesus is always sweet to everyone with the exception of two instances. First, when the money changers and the merchants had made a flea market out of His Father's house, which I can fully understand, but the next was a fight Jesus picks with the Pharisees, in Matt 23:33. This puzzled me at first, but when I began to meditate upon it, God showed me that it was time for the cross, and Jesus was doing what He needed to do to move them to do what was already in their hearts.

Many secular books have been written about the explosive power of words. Where do you think that came from? Jesus said it 2,000 years ago. I can recall, before I got saved, as a secular martial arts instructor giving speeches to my students about the power of positive speaking and I don't even know where I heard it, I just knew it was helpful. And without knowing why, I knew that anytime I overheard a student say something like, "I'm no good," or "I'll never be able to do this or that," I would always interrupt them and make them change their words. How would I possibly know to do that, and why?

Ironically enough, knowing what I now know and having been instructed by God Himself about the power of words, I can honestly say that it is more difficult, now, as a mature believer, with all the information and experience I have, to never say anything that might be used against me by the Evil One. I imagine it's because Satan has positioned one of his more persuasive demons against me. When you reach a new level, you come up against a new and more powerful devil. Either that or I'm just noticing it a lot more now than I did before. I suspect it's a little bit of both.

We desperately need to surround ourselves with other believers that will help us when we are down, correct our words when we misspeak, and remind us of the promises of God, when we forget. Let me encourage you to find at least one person that you can be accountable to... somebody that will watch your spiritual back, as you watch theirs. Obviously, this position is best reserved for your spouse, but if you are not married or if your spouse is not where you are spiritually, find somebody that can fill the position. It's paramount!

I know it sounds over the top, but you cannot afford to connect yourselves any longer with ignorant people that do not understand these things. Their ignorance can literally kill you, because of who you are and what you now know. And unfortunately, you cannot unlearn what you have already learned here. There is no going back now, so you might as well reason within your heart to go after this thing with everything you have. Become the person you were created to be, and stop limping through life half asleep.

It is, also, important that you do not go and get offended when a brother or sister in Christ corrects your words. I have seen the Devil use this tactic against believers by causing it to become competitive and petty as one gets offended when their friend brings something to their attention. This is not a competition. Remember to do all things with love, and if your only source of accountability is easily offended, because of immaturity when you encourage them to watch their words, ask the Lord instead to reveal it to them and pray for their maturity.

In this world we are constantly moving in and out of hundreds of lives, saved and unsaved, mature and childlike, and it is imperative that we figure out how to navigate our way, so that we edify them with our deeds and our words of encouragement. You know that you are doing well when you leave people better off than they were when you first met.

Jesus gives us a fabulous explanation of the power of suggestion in Matt 6. Most versions of the Bible mistranslate it as,

> **Do not worry then, saying, What will we eat? Or What will we drink? Or What will we wear for clothing?** Matt 6:31

The sense was that people worry about such things and Jesus is telling them not to worry, because God's got their back. That's not entirely wrong, but it is, actually, much deeper than that. The King James version words it correctly when it says,

> **Therefore take no thought, saying, What shall we eat? or, What shall we drink? or, Wherewithal shall we be clothed?**

The difference is this: Satan places the thought in your head in hopes to get you to say it, because if you say it, you give up your Authority and He can then run to the court of the Throne and accuse us. If you don't think that Satan can present himself before the Lord then you must not have read the book of Job:

> **Now there was a day when the sons of God came to present themselves before the Lord, and Satan was among them. And the Lord said to Satan, From where do you come? So Satan answered the Lord and said, From going to and fro on the earth and walking back and forth on it.** Job 1:6-7

Another example is in the book of Revelation:

> *... for the accuser of our brothers has been thrown down, who accuses them day and night before our God.* Rev. 12:10

Therefore, Jesus is telling us not to give up our Authority to Satan by repeating His lies when He said, *Take no thought saying.* Remember Mark 11:23, *You will have whatever you say, either for, or against you.* The negative thought you are hearing is just your enemy trying to get you to repeat it. Oh, and here's a tip, stop talking to yourself.

One day in 2005 my wife, Angela, began complaining of headaches, but this was not just any ordinary headache, as she went through an entire bottle of 500 milligram Tylenol in a weekend and it didn't even put a dent in it. Monday, she went to the doctor, who assumed it was a migraine or something and he prescribed a very strong pain killer, which I believe was codeine-Tylenol. It had absolutely no effect on her pain, whatsoever, so by Thursday she contacted a doctor friend of ours and he scheduled an MRI. She was in agony.

Sitting in his office, looking at the results, he turned to her and said, "Angela, I'm so sorry, but your Myelin Sheath has deteriorated. I have seen this about a dozen times. Nobody knows what causes it, and there is no cure. You are going to die. Very soon all your nerves will begin to react strangely, and all your muscles will start twitching and moving involuntarily. In about 2 or 3 months all your muscles will begin to fail, then your organs will shut down one by one, then paralysis will set in and then death." Being a good friend of ours, he had tears in his eyes as he tried to comfort her saying, "I'm so sorry Angela, there is nothing we can do." She just sat there for a few seconds, not saying a word. Suddenly, she arose and said, "I rebuke that in the name of Jesus. My God has not brought me through everything He has, just to let me die like this. I am a Child of the Most High God, an heir to the throne and I am seated in Heavenly places with Christ Jesus. No weapon formed against me shall prosper and every tongue that rises against me, I condemn in the name of Jesus. And I condemn that prognosis, in Jesus name." With that, she turned and walked out. Speechless, our friend tried calling and texting her, but she ignored all of his attempts.

She said that, as soon as, she left his office, every symptom he described began to manifest itself. All her nerves and muscles began to twitch and move erratically. When she arrived at our business, visibly shaken, our receptionist, a spirit-filled believer, asked her if she was ok. Being careful not to condemn herself with her words, she said, "I just received a negative report from the doctor and I'm asking God for a Word to stand on in faith." Immediately, Susan said she felt like she heard a word and opened her Bible to it. I do not recall what it was, but whatever it was, it spoke to Angela and she stood on that as her Word from God. They read it, prayed together, and stood in faith. Two weeks later, her phone rings and it was our doctor friend, the same one that Angela had been avoiding. She forgot to screen this call and just picked it up. Surprised he got through to her, he pleaded with her to at least get a second opinion. She paused for a second and said, "Ok, I'll get a second opinion, but not for me, I'll do it for you."

Sitting in his office again, this time looking at two MRI's, the first on the left and the second on the right, the doctor seemed flustered. He could not understand how the first MRI showed a conclusive deterioration in her Myelin Sheath, but in the second one, it was perfectly normal. Puzzled, he asked what she had done. With confidence, she said, "I told you, I am a Child of God, and these signs will follow all who believe in the name of Jesus." At that, she got up and walked out. Interesting side note, she never told me about it when it happened. I only learned about it when I overheard her telling it as a testimony to an employee, who had just received a bad report. By not accepting the prognosis and repeating it, she never gave up her Authority, and therefore, it never had the legal right to afflict her.

If the doctor calls a Child of God, a believer, and tells them that the test results are in and they conclusively show multiple sclerosis or cancer, or whatever is present, that disease does not have the legal right to be there. That is, unless that person, calls their spouse or a friend or a relative and says, "I have multiple sclerosis," or "I have cancer." If they claim it, it is theirs. They have just given the disease the legal right, the Authority to be there. Remember what Jesus said, *Take no thought saying.* Once you say it, you take it. It is yours, and you own it.

This does not mean that we act like we are in denial. If blood work comes back showing a disease is present, the facts of the matter is, the blood work proves it is present. There are facts and there is the truth. The fact is, the blood work is showing the cancer. The truth is, the cancer has no Authority over you, and therefore, does not have the legal right to stay, unless you give it your Authority by claiming it. We are not delusional. We are not ignoring the facts, which are very real, but they are not more real than the truth.

So what do we do? What can we say when we receive a bad report? Whatever you do, you do not want to take the thought by saying it. You do not want to claim ownership of it. You could call your spouse and say, "Honey, the blood work shows cancer is present." You have not claimed it or taken ownership. You are simply stating a fact. The fact is, the blood work shows cancer is present, but the truth is, it has no Authority to stay, and you have the Authority to command it to bow to the name of Jesus and go. How do I know? Because I have done exactly that on three different occasions, with The Altar of Love. In every case, the cancer has completely gone. Three out of three. God is batting a 1,000.

Angela never gave her Authority away, therefore, it had no legal right to stay. If you recall, she did begin to experience all the symptoms of twitching nerves and muscle spasms. That is how the Devil works. Remember, He is like batman. He's got lots of gadgets and parlor tricks all designed to get her to say it, so he could harvest her Authority through her words. The power He has is the power we give him with the words we speak, and that power is our Superpower called Authority.

If the believer has engaged in behavior that resulted in that disease being there, like a sexually transmitted disease, because of adultery or fornication, then Authority was given to the disease already. This was one of the awesome things I learned in The Altar of Love. By all means, watch your words, but the dynamics change. In order to remove it, its Authority to stay must be removed first, then the disease can be removed. We will cover this process later in the chapter called, **Restoring a Believer's Authority**.

Another way to look at it, is as a football analogy. The running back, with the ball, is approached by the defensive player, attempting to tackle him. The defensive player wraps his arms around the waist of the running back and attempts to tackle him. It is possible for the running back to break free of the tackle, but it is difficult, and not likely. Likewise, if you have given your Authority to the Devil by claiming it already, it is not impossible to get your Authority back, it just requires knowledge of how to and the faith to believe it is done.

Conversely, there is a strategy, a move the running back can apply when a defender attempts to tackle him, called a stiff arm. A stiff arm is when the running back extends his arm fully, placing his palm against the helmet of the defender, thus keeping him at a distance far enough away that the defender cannot wrap his arms around the running backs waist. The best the defender can do is grasp at the running backs arm, but that will not provide him the leverage to take a strong running back to the ground. This is a symbol of watching your words; you never give the enemy the leverage to take you down. That sickness, that disease never really gets a hold of you. The symptoms never really reach their potential and it just seems to fizzle out.

In Daniel 10, God reveals to us the events that go on behind the scenes when we pray. *In those days I, Daniel, was mourning three full weeks, saying, I ate no pleasant food, no meat or wine came into my mouth, nor did I anoint myself at all, till three whole weeks were fulfilled. Now on the twenty-fourth day of the first month, as I was by the side of the great river, that is, the Tigris, I lifted my eyes and looked, and behold, a certain man clothed in linen, whose waist was girded with gold of Uphaz His body was like beryl, his face like the appearance of lightning, his eyes like torches of fire, his arms and feet like burnished bronze in color, and the sound of his words like the voice of a multitude.*

And I, Daniel, alone saw the vision, for the men who were with me did not see the vision; but a great terror fell upon them, so that they fled to hide themselves. Therefore I was left alone when I saw this great vision, and no strength remained in me; for my vigor was turned to frailty in me, and I retained no strength. Yet I heard the sound of his words; and while I heard the sound of his words, I was in a deep sleep on my face, with my face to the ground.

Suddenly, a hand touched me, which made me tremble on my knees and on the palms of my hands. And he said to me, "O Daniel, man greatly beloved, understand the words that I speak to you, and stand upright, for I have now been sent to you." While he was speaking this word to me, I stood trembling.

Then he said to me, "Do not fear, Daniel, for from the first day that you set your heart to understand, and to humble yourself before your God, your words were heard; and I have come because of your words. But the prince of Persia withstood me twenty-one days; and behold, Michael, one of the chief princes, came to help me, for I had been left alone there with the kings of Persia.

There are a few really important things to consider here. First, Daniel prayed and fasted, but it took 21 days before the angel of the Lord showed up. Daniel's attitude is like, Dude, what took so long? The angel responds and says, "Don't even go their Daniel, because from the moment you set your heart to seek the Lord, He sent me." As soon as we petition the Lord, He sends our answer. The angel goes on to say, "And I have come, because of your words." This is where it gets interesting, because the implication here is that Daniel never doubted that the answer was coming even though it had taken 21 days. Regardless of the delay, Daniel continued to believe in faith and that fact was evident when the angel says, "Because of your words."

Satan knows us well enough to know that if He can just cause a little delay, we will begin to doubt, and as we already learned, *a man who doubts is a double-minded man, let him expect nothing from God.* Satan knows this, so He sends up a roadblock to cause a delay, then He posts a demon in your ear to tell you God is not going to answer your prayer. It probably sounds something like this, "See? You prayed and nothing happened. He must not have heard you," or "Sometimes He does and sometimes He doesn't. I guess he's not answering today." The truth is, you prayed, He sent an answer immediately and Satan sent a roadblock to create a delay and went to work on you to get you to doubt. Daniel's **words** did not stop his answer, because he continued to speak in faith even though he did not see it. That's it, in a nutshell. The power the Devil has, is the power we give him by the words we speak. Daniel never gave Satan his power, his Authority.

Chapter Six

The Power of God's Word:

Leg 3, Part 2 of The Altar of Love

Words are things, containers of power that can create or destroy.

Now faith is the substance of things hoped for, the evidence of things not seen. For by it the elders obtained a good testimony. By faith we understand that the worlds were framed by the Word of God, so that the things which are seen were not made of things which are visible. Heb 11:1-3

Clearly he is saying that invisible words create visible things. **Things,** Strong's G4229 – pragma (*prag'-mah*) a material object. By definition, these invisible things we call words are actually material objects. The Word of God creates **Things,** pragma, material objects in the spirit realm, which then manifests themselves in the natural realm through our faith. Nothing happens in the natural realm until it happens in the spirit realm first. That is why Jesus uses the parable of a farmer planting seeds, to explain how this spiritual law of the spoken Word of God works. Just because we do not see words, does not mean they do not have substance. A good example would be radio waves. Just because we can't see them, doesn't mean they're not there.

Let's go back to Heb 11:1, *Now faith is the substance of things hoped for, the evidence of things not seen.* Faith is the substance of the things we are hoping for, the things we have been believing God for. Much as flour is the substance of a cake, faith is the substance of the thing you've been praying for..."The evidence of things not seen." If evidence is proof of a thing, then the evidence that you have that thing you've been believing in, is the fact that you cannot see it. That's faith, it's believing in something you cannot see. It's not faith if you have to see it to believe it. What Paul is saying here is this: The very fact that you cannot see the thing you are hoping to get from God is the proof that you already have it. WHAT?

So your friend calls you up and asks if you have gotten an answer to the thing you've praying about and you tell him, "Yes I have." "Oh, that's awesome, can I come over and see it?" "No," you reply. "Why not?" they ask. "Because it isn't here yet," you say. "But I thought you said that you have it," they say. "I do, it just isn't here yet," you reply. They reply, "If it isn't here, how do you know you have it, where's the evidence?" You answer them saying, "The fact that I can't see it is the evidence that I have it. That's what the Word says."

Listen to me carefully. You did not get your miracle the day it showed up, the day you saw it manifest itself. You got your miracle the day you set your heart to find your answer in the Word of God, the day you found the verse, the scripture that pertained to your situation, the day you confessed that Word out of your mouth and the day you believed in your heart by faith that it was done. That's the day you got your miracle, and I can prove it in the Word.

Mary is visited by the angel that tells her she is going to have a baby, but Mary asks the angel, "How is that possible seeing how I have never 'known' a man?" The Greek word for 'known,' describes an intimate, sexual relationship. What Mary is actually saying is, "How is that possible? I've never had sex with a man." The angel says, "The Holy Spirit will come upon you, and the power of the Most High will overshadow you, therefore, also, that Holy One who is to be born will be called the Son of God... For with God nothing is impossible." Then Mary said, "Let it be unto me according to your word." That is the moment that Mary conceived, the moment she believed the Rhema Word in her heart and spoke it with her mouth.

Let's contrast that with Mary's cousin Elizabeth, who is to give birth to John the Baptist. The angel, Gabriel, goes to her husband Zachariah and tells him pretty much the same thing he told Mary. But all Zachariah did was complain and doubt, so Gabriel made him mute from that minute until after the birth of John, because Gabriel knew that Zachariah could not control his words.

Mary believed on blind faith alone. Furthermore, what was being told to her had never happened before. There was no record of anyone being impregnated in the history of Israel, so that had to make it more difficult for her, but her faith was so strong and she believed unto pregnancy.

When Jesus was fasting in the desert for 40 days and the Devil tempted Him three times, what did Jesus do? He said, *It is written.* Jesus doesn't argue with the Devil, He just quotes God's Word. Whatever your situation, you must find the Word of God that specifically deals with your trial and speak that Word. Then, you stand in faith without wavering until it comes to pass, regardless of how long it takes. Abraham waited 20 years for his son Isaac. The absolute best illustration of this principle is in Mark 4, The Parable of the Sower. In the Parable of the Sower, Jesus makes one of His most profound statements of the New Testament, and it is my opinion, that it is the key to all spiritual wisdom.

Mighty bold statement, I know, but just stay with me here. *Then Jesus said to them, Do you not understand this parable? Then how will you understand any of the parables?* Mark 4:13

In other words, If you don't get this, you're not going to understand anything I teach you. So, just how important is the parable of the sower? It's the most important lesson of all. It is the key to spiritual wisdom. For if you do not understand the Parable of the Sower, you will not understand anything that Jesus is teaching. As well, every lesson, every teaching, every study either comes out of, or goes back to the sower, in one way or another.

In the Parable of the Sower, Jesus is describing how the Kingdom of God operates. He tells of a farmer that is sowing seeds and the four different things that happen to, and as a result of, the seed that is sown. After hearing the parable, the disciples come to Jesus and inquire of the understanding. Jesus responds by telling them why He speaks in parables.

To you has been given to know the mysteries of the Kingdom of God, but to those who are outside, everything is done in parables... Mark 4:13

Jesus is telling them that the purpose of the parables is to hide the knowledge of spiritual things from the Devil. Paul confirms this in 1 Corinthians 2.

We speak the hidden wisdom of God in a mystery, which God ordained before the ages for our glory. Which none of the rulers of this age understood. For if they had, they would not have crucified the Lord of glory. 1 Corinthians 2:7-8

Parables are nothing more that spiritual nuggets of Godly wisdom hidden in a superficial story. Because the Holy spirit is inside us, it is within our ability to understand the parables. Satan does not have the Spirit of God, and therefore, He never understood what Jesus was saying. Let me give you a great example:

The Parable of the Good Samaritan

Then Jesus answered and said: *"A certain man went down from Jerusalem to Jericho, and fell among thieves, who stripped him of his clothing, wounded him, and departed, leaving him half dead. Now by chance, a certain priest came down that road. And when he saw him, he passed by on the other side. Likewise, a Levite, when he arrived at the place, came and looked, and passed by on the other side. But a certain Samaritan, as he journeyed, came where he was. And when he saw him, he had compassion. So he went to him and bandaged his wounds, pouring on oil and wine; and he set him on his own animal, brought him to an inn, and took care of him. On the next day, when he departed, he took out two denarii, gave them to the innkeeper, and said to him, "Take care of him; and whatever more you spend, when I come again, I will repay you."*

Meaning of the Good Samaritan

If you go to any church in the world, they will tell you how it is a lesson of being kind to thy neighbor, or do unto others as you would have them do unto you, but that is the surface meaning designed to hide the real meaning. Remember, the wisdom of God is spiritually discerned. The certain man traveling from Jerusalem represents Adam. The band of thieves represents Satan and his demons, that left us separated from God and dying spiritually. The priest and the Levite represent the 613 laws of Moses and all the ritual sacrifices that could not save us. The Good Samaritan is Jesus, who saved us and left us at the inn. The inn is the Holy Spirit that keeps us until His return. The Samaritan paid the price of two denarii and said, "If costs more, I'll pay it when I return." A denarii was one days wage, so Jesus paid him two days wage. One day is as 1,000 years, so 2 denarii would be 2,000 years. Jesus was saying He'd be back in approximately 2,000 years. This is a picture of the world from Adam to present, as well as, a general timing of His return. I like how Jesus allowed himself some wiggle, room for a delay in his return.

So let's go through the sower and figure out why Jesus said all wisdom begins here. The sower is a picture of the world, which is really divided into two parts, the saved and the unsaved. Jesus only briefly touches on the unsaved, so His main focus of this parable is on people that recognize who He is, because, let's face it, not everyone does. He breaks them down into three groups, and if you've been doing this for any length of time, you can see how accurate it really is. All Christians will fit into one of these 3 categories.

The Parable of the Sower

Listen! Behold, a sower went out to sow. And it happened, as he sowed, that some seed fell by the wayside; and the birds of the air came and devoured it. Some fell on stony ground, where it did not have much earth; and immediately it sprang up, because it had no depth of earth. But when the sun was up it was scorched, and because it had no root it withered away.

And some seed fell among thorns; and the thorns grew up and choked it, and it yielded no crop. But other seed fell on good ground and yielded a crop that sprang up, increased and produced: some thirtyfold, some sixty, and some a hundred.

The Parable of the Sower Explained

And He said to them, *Do you not understand this parable? How then will you understand all the parables? The sower sows the word. And these are the ones by the wayside where the word is sown. When they hear, Satan comes immediately and takes away the word that was sown in their hearts. These, likewise, are the ones sown on stony ground who, when they hear the word, immediately receive it with gladness; and they have no root in themselves, and so endure only for a time. Afterward, when tribulation or persecution arises for the word's sake, immediately they stumble. Now, these are the ones sown among thorns; they are the ones who hear the word, and the cares of this world, the deceitfulness of riches, and the desires for other things entering in choke the word, and it becomes unfruitful. But these are the ones sown on good ground, those who hear the word, accept it, and bear fruit: some thirtyfold, some sixty, and some a hundred.*

The Sower is the person who is preaching or teaching the Word of God. The soil is the heart, and the seed is the word of God. The ones sown on the wayside do not get saved, we know this, because Jesus tells the same parable in Luke, but in it He says, lest they get saved. Obviously then, the ones on the wayside never get it, and notice that Satan came immediately to eat the seed, which is the Word of God that was sown in their heart. This, also, proves that there must be a demon posted by us at all times, ready to devour the seed, the Word of God, that is being sown.

Also, notice the condition of their heart. Jesus compares this man's heart to the wayside. The wayside was the hardened path the farmer walked up and down upon, as he planted seed to his left and right. Remember, it was not like it is now. All they had was oxen, not tractors. They walked up and down hardened paths called, the wayside, as they planted the seed. It was so hard that the seed just sat on top and could not take root. The birds, who represent the demons, came and ate the seed.

Next are the ones sown among rocks. These people get saved and are on fire for God, but only for a short time. As soon as the trials come, they fall away, because they have rocks in their heart and the Word does not make a good root, because the soil is not very good. For a plant to be healthy, the root must be strong, for a root to be strong, the soil must be soft and fertile. If the soil is your heart, it is up to you to prepare your heart the same way a farmer prepares his soil, with loving care.

Let's say you have two farmers, side by side. The first one takes his plot of land and cuts down the trees, cleans out the weeds, and plants his seed. The second farmer cuts the trees, digs up the stumps, cleans out the weeds, removes all the rocks, tills the soil, adds fertilizer, tills it again, and adds gypsum, which softens the soil and improves the pH. Then he tills it one last time, so it is ready to receive seed. Whose land will produce a better crop. Obviously, the one who lovingly cared for his soil. This is a picture of the condition of our hearts, and if you are the farmer, then it is your responsibility to prepare your heart, your soil to receive the Word of God.

After I got saved, Angela was still in the world and it was a very difficult time for us, because of that. I began praying, and asking God to change her, to get her saved and filled with the Holy Spirit, and as clear as a bell, I heard, ***You worry about you and I will take care of her, she's my responsibility.*** Immediately, I saw all the junk in me that needed to be removed. All the rocks that were in my heart that needed to be cleaned out. From that day forward, my prayer changed to, Help me improve my, attitude, my behavior. Help me to clean my heart, so that I am righteousness of you Father in Christ Jesus. It was only about a year or two later that she began to draw near to the Lord, and I know it was because of the change she saw in me.

The rocks symbolize all the past pain, traumas, disappointments, abuses, etc., that we hold onto and are unable or unwilling to forgive. The sun that scorches the plant indicates trials and tribulations that happen in life. As soon as adversity came, immediately the ones with rocks in their heart stumbled. That word 'stumble' means 'to get offended.' They got offended and went back to the world. "I'm done with that Christianity stuff. The preacher said I'd have my best life now, but ever since I got saved, it's gone to hell in a hand basket." Maybe they got offended, because they weren't properly greeted at church, or the pastor was too busy to talk to them, or nobody asked them for prayer. Satan will use just about anything. He's known you since you were born. He knows all the rocks that are in your heart and most of them are there because of Him. He knows just how to offend you, how to get the one person to say the one thing that will make you explode. He's been at it for 6,000 years, and He's a pro.

When I realized that I was supposed to start preaching a few years ago, I thought I would follow the proper protocol. Because I was attending, really more like hiding, in this little church, I wanted to let the pastor know what I believed the Lord was telling me. I didn't want to go out and start competing with his church. I liked the people there. Maybe, I thought I'd do it under their covering. I'm not really sure what I was thinking, but this felt like the right thing to do. After just one meeting with him, he determined that I was unfit to teach the Word. Don't ask me why. Maybe he was going through stuff of his own, maybe the church had issues with the eldership, maybe he just misjudged me. Whatever the case, I didn't get offended or hold it against him and I didn't stop attending there, until God called me to assist at another church. You see, I know my Identity. I know how and when my Father is talking to me. My value was not in anything the pastor said or thought about me. It is always in what my Father thinks and says about me.

In the parable of the sower, the ones sown among rocks, for whatever reason, got offended and stopped going and slowly slid back into the world. I think it is important that we take a moment and discuss the grave danger of offense. When John the Baptist was imprisoned, he called his disciples to him and told them to go ask Jesus if He was really the Messiah, or were they supposed to be looking for another. You really need to see and understand the enormity of this offense. John and Jesus were cousins, and only six months apart. It is customary for Jewish families to gather and celebrate all the feasts, together. Therefore, even if they lived apart, Jesus and John would have seen each other seven or eight times a year for days on end, their entire life.

Being only six months apart and cut from the same cloth, surely they played and hung out together. John's mother, Elizabeth, knew that Jesus was the Messiah. She said as much to Mary when Mary went to visit her when they were both pregnant. John's mother must have been telling John who Jesus was his whole life. Then, John recognizes Jesus as the Messiah when Jesus shows up to get baptized. Didn't John say, "Behold the lamb of God..." Next, John is standing next to Jesus as the voice of God Himself says, **Behold My Son, in whom I am well pleased.** Clearly, John knows who Jesus is, so why did he send his disciples to ask Jesus if they should look for another?

Because John got offended. He must have been thinking to himself, Dude, I'm your cousin. You're the Messiah. Why won't you get me out of prison? So, Jesus is preaching when John's disciples come to Him and say, "John sent us to ask you, are You the One or should we be looking for another?" Jesus doesn't even respond to them directly, but looks at the crowd and says, **Woe to you because of offenses.** Do you understand the magnitude of the word 'woe?' Woe is like saying, "Uh oh, you're in a very dangerous place here." It means, great dread is on the horizon. And, well... what happened to John? He was beheaded.

Now, let's contrast that with the way Peter and Paul handled their time in prison. They were full of joy, sang songs, prayed for the other prisoners and even the guards. Earthquakes broke open the prison doors, the guards fell asleep, angels escorted them out, and whole platoons of guards got saved. Completely different results, to completely opposite responses to a similar situation. Therefore, when Jesus says, in the sower, they got offended, He's saying, because of their offense, they are now in jeopardy of great dread. Because if they go back into the world, their salvation literally hangs in the balance. Why? Because, in Matthew 24:13, Jesus said, *But the one who perseveres to the end will be saved.* The definition of the word Persevere is Strong's #5278 hypoménō - **to hold fast to one's faith in Christ.** Absolutely and emphatically, under misfortunes and trials, with no wavering.

Going back to the world is not exactly holding fast to one's faith in Christ. You will, also, notice regarding the ones sown among rocks, it says that Satan came to steal the Word that was sown in their hearts. Satan is after the Word, because He knows how powerful it is. He knows if the Word gets in you, it will eventually come out of you and just like Jesus in the desert. If the Word comes out of your mouth, it will defeat the Devil.

> *The things that come out of the mouth, come from the heart.* Matthew 15:8

As I said before, nothing comes out of a man's mouth except for what is in his heart. Nothing goes in your heart except what you see and hear. A tree is known by its fruit. If a person is vulgar, rude, insulting, insensitive or hurtful, that's what is in their heart. It's a good indication that they do not read their Word, and most likely they have no intimate relationship with the Lord. This is precisely why, as parents, we must monitor what TV shows our children see and what music they listen to. A person's heart, their treasure, is made up of their environment. If your environment is trash, everything you see and hear is trash. If trash goes in you all day, trash will eventually come out. If you soak up dirty water with a sponge, when you squeeze the sponge, dirty water is coming out. It's the same principle.

The ones sown among thorns are more mature believers that made it through the original trials, because they cared for their soil, the heart. It is our responsibility to guard our heart and make sure no bitterness unforgiveness, or offense, is allowed to enter. Otherwise, it will fester and grow. We will only go, as far as, the condition of our heart will take us.

> *Be angry, yet do not sin. Do not let the sun set upon your anger, and do not give the Devil a foothold.* Ephesians 4:27

God understands that we may get on each other's nerves, occasionally. However, if we do get angry, we are instructed not to take it to bed, because the Devil will use it against you. That is exactly the foothold He needs to destroy a relationship. That is the Authority He is looking for to gain entrance. If you find yourself so upset about a situation that you are literally waking up angry, woe to you, for great dread is on the horizon. For your own sake, forgive.

> *Therefore, if you are offering your gift at The Altar and remember that if your brother has something against you… First go and be reconciled to your brother; then come and offer your gift.* Matthew 5:23

Jesus is saying, if you only knew just how things worked in the spirit realm, you'd stop what you are doing and run immediately to make up with your adversary. Regardless of who's right or wrong, doing so benefits you, because it keeps the rocks out of your heart. Holding grudges and unforgiveness only hurts you by giving up your Authority, which gives opportunity to the Devil to enter you and remain until you repent, confess, and evict. The foul creatures will eventually bring sickness and disease to destroy you.

If we choose to hold on to past hurts and failures, we are doomed to flame out, as in the parable of the sower. However, if you let go of the things of the past, and the present for that matter, and carefully guard your heart, you put yourself in a place where your Father can use you and the adversary will fear you. If you walk in love and forgiveness, it will be well with you all the days of your life.

Regarding the group sown among thorns, a period of time has elapsed. The Devil is experienced, and patiently waits, 5, 10, 15, or even 20 years, allowing you to grow comfortable, fat, wealthy, and happy, and then he makes his move. Mark 4:19 says, *The cares of the world, the deceitfulness of riches, and the desire for other things, enter in and choke the Word and it became unfruitful.*

1 John 2, describes this part perfectly,

> *For all that is in the world, the lust of the flesh and the lust of the eyes and the boastful pride of life, is not from the Father, but is from the world.* 1 John 2:16

The Bible says that Jesus was tempted in every way as we are: Lust of the flesh, lust of the eyes, and the pride of life.

'The cares of the world' – Cares, merimna (mer-im-nah); Strong's #3308; to divide the mind. The word denotes distractions, anxieties, burdens, and worries. Merimna means to be anxious about daily life. Such worry is unnecessary, because the Father provides for both our daily needs and our special needs. Philippians 4:6 *Be anxious for nothing...* (don't worry about anything, ever)

'Deceitfulness of riches' – Prosperity gospel, Pride of life (1 John 2:16)

'Desire of other things' – Lusts of the flesh & Lust of the eyes (1 John 2:16)

If you compare Satan's strategy between the seed sown among rocks to the seed sown among thorns, you will notice one interesting difference. The trials and tribulations that come against the ones sown among rocks, come from outside sources, things that are happening to them outside of their control. In the ones sown among thorns, "The cares of the world, the deceitfulness of riches, and the desire for other things enter in." These things are now on the inside of you. Your destruction is coming from the inside now. These are the things that Satan has either planted in your heart over the past few years or things He has noticed about your heart, while observing you. Therefore, this lesson of purging your heart of rocks becomes even more important as you mature in our Christian walk. Cleaning you heart is a lifelong process.

The last group, the ones sown on "good ground," signifies one who has fed the spirit faithfully by reading the Word - *study to show yourself approved, praying - Praying always with all prayer and supplication in the spirit, and continually standing in faith - Be a doer of the Word, not a hearer only.* Some 30, some 60 and others 100 fold represent those who feed the spirit more, will have more yield in their harvest than those that feed the spirit less. Obviously, those who spend more time in the Word feeding their spirit will receive a greater gain. The Parable of the Sower is a beautiful illustration of God's Word as it relates to the condition of our heart. If you want a good crop, make sure your heart is purged of all rocks and watch out for weeds.

The Parable of the Growing Seed

And He said, The Kingdom of God is as if a man should scatter seed on the ground, and should sleep by night and rise by day, and the seed should sprout and grow, he himself does not know how. For the earth yields crops by itself: first the blade, then the head, after that the full grain in the head. But when the grain ripens, immediately he puts in the sickle, because the harvest has come.

Jesus begins the parable by saying, *The Kingdom of God is as if.* He is saying that this parable is an illustration of how the principle of sowing God's Word like a seed actually works. And let me add that the actual sowing of the Word is not more important than the attitude we have afterwards. Jesus said, *In this world you will have tribulation.* He didn't say that everything was going to be hunky-dory. He said we'd have tribulation. When the tribulation arises, the sower sows the Word. Like the farmer, we find the Word that deals with our situation and speak it with our mouth. Now, notice what the farmer does after he has sown the Word of God; he goes to sleep. He does not lay awake worried or wondering if the seed will sprout, because he knows if the seed has sun, water, and the soil is good, he will get a crop. We have to have that same attitude when we sow the Word of God.

Our attitude is the key here, and if you think about it, we really only have three options:

1) We can adopt the same attitude as the farmer, sow the Word of God over our situation, go about our days and nights as usual without worry or doubt, and expect the Word to grow like a seed until it produces a crop.

2) We can sow the Word, complain it's taking too long, worry whether or not it's going to happen at all, or speak negatively that it has not happened in the way or time we want.

3) Don't sow any Word and just take our chances in the natural realm. If you are wondering why I would even offer this ridiculous option, it's because it's the most common response among Christians. Do nothing and hand your Authority away.

It is better to trust God than to put confidence in man. Ps. 118:8

When Jesus reached up to get a fig off the tree that had no figs, He cursed it. That tree did not immediately wither and die. They went into town and came back a day or so later and that's when they noticed it was dead. It took time for the Word to kill the root. Herein lies the real lesson of the sower: the Word we sow is not just dealing with the surface symptoms, the things that appear to be the problem, but really are not. No, the problem you are having most likely has a spiritual root and the Word you have sown is doing a much bigger job than you can see with your natural eyes. It is going to the root of the cause. it must first kill the root, otherwise, the problem will remain.

This principle is the very thing God was teaching me when He showed me The Altar of Love. When I was praying for healing for people, I was only dealing with the symptom of the problem. One day at the gym, I was told by the Holy spirit to pray for a young lady. When I noticed that she was absolutely

147

gorgeous, I didn't do it. I brushed it off like I didn't really hear it. She was so pretty, I didn't want to bother her. Attractive women get harassed terribly at the gym, and I didn't want to be just another guy that she has to get rid of.

As I prepared to do a set of lat pull-downs, I clearly heard the voice of the Lord say it again, **_Pray for her._** This time I could not deny that it was the Holy Spirit, but I contended with Him and stood my ground. I said to myself, I don't want to interrupt her, so I reached up to grab the bar when I hear, **PRAY FOR HER!** like He was yelling at me. I actually apologized, chuckled to myself, and walked around the machine to approach her. Sure enough, when she realized I was focused on her, she kind of rolled her eyes, not blatantly, but I noticed it.

Now I'm having a conversation with the Father, and I'm telling Him, You see, that's what I was afraid of. Why would you do this to me? But I'm nothing, if not obedient, so I told her, I didn't ask her. I told her that she needed prayer for something and she starts crying. Immediately, all her defenses went down and she said, "Yes, please." I asked her what for, and she said that all her organs were shutting down... she was dying. You would have never known by looking at her, that she was going to die soon. As soon as I began to pray, I saw roots coming from all of her organs, going upward and fading away. I stopped, let go of her hand and told her the shutting down of her organs was just the symptom of a much bigger problem, there was a root cause to her issue. She confirmed that Word and said she was diagnosed with Endometriosis. At that time I had heard of Endometriosis, but I really didn't know what it was, but now that I know what I'm dealing with, I can address the root cause. I asked her, what was the one symptom that she dealt with every day that, if gone, would prove to her she was healed, and she said, "Pain." She was in excruciating constant pain. She could barely cope with daily life, because the pain was so intense.

Remember, I'm not praying for God to heal her. I have the legal right to assume Authority over Endometriosis, because she has submitted to me. I start speaking to the spirit that has ushered in this disease and I'm commanding it to go, then I start speaking to the disease itself and I command it to die at the root. I spoke to every organ in her body, one by one and I commanded them to come alive. I commanded them to function normally, as when they were created by Jesus Himself. Next, I spoke to the pain, because pain is a separate entity all by itself.

I commanded the pain to go in the name of Jesus, and let me emphasize this point... while I am taking Authority, I'm doing it in the name of Jesus. I, actually, have no Authority at all on my own, but whatever I bind on Earth, He will bind in Heaven. This prayer took more than a few minutes, because there was so much to cover. When I was done, I opened my eyes and she was staring at me with tears running down her cheeks. I asked her if she had any pain, and with a big smile, she said, "No, not even a little bit." She was completely healed and later confided in me that she had no idea why, but she felt compelled to go to the gym that day even though she was in horrible pain.

We have to trust our Father, that He has our best interest at heart, that He understands our situation, and that He really cares about the things that concern us.

__The Lord will cease that which concerns me…__ Psalm 138:8

In other words, He makes it stop. Look at it from God's point of view. Jesus is virtually telling us in the parable of the sower, that this process of sowing God's Word is how the Kingdom of God operates.

If you want to get the same results as Jesus, you have to follow the pattern of the farmer here. Yet, almost nobody in the world understands how important the sower is and how it works. Only a handful of people on this planet recognize the principle of the sower and follow it faithfully. How do you think your Father will react if you are one of the few who will trust Him? I'm assuming He's going to be mighty proud of you.

__For the eyes of the LORD roam throughout the whole earth to show Himself strong on behalf of those whose heart is fully devoted to him.__ 2 Chronicles 16:9

He's actively looking for people that will sow His Word and stand in faith, regardless of how their circumstances look.

__For as the rain comes down, and the snow from Heaven, And do not return there, But water the earth, And make it bring forth and bud, That it may give seed to the sower And bread to the eater, So shall My word be that goes forth from My mouth; It shall not return to Me void, But it shall accomplish what I please, And it shall prosper in the thing for which I sent it.__ Isaiah 55:10-11

This verse only serves to confirm the parable of the sower and God Himself gives us an illustration of how this Word seed works. Because Jesus is no longer in the flesh upon the Earth,

God needs a human to speak His Word through. When we speak God's Word out of our mouth, it does not return to God void. Void implies uselessness, emptiness, or an inability to accomplish some object's intended purpose. God says that His Word will not return useless, but it will accomplish what He pleases. This is not a maybe or possibly, He says it will prosper in the thing, for which, it was sent.

> *For you have magnified your word even above your own name.* Ps. 138:2

This shows just how important His Word is to Him. So, we have the name of Jesus, which is above every name that is named, but God is saying that His Word is so revered, so special, so important that He will exalt it even above His own name. Why? Because God is not a man that He can lie. If it says it in His Word, then He is obligated to perform it. If he does not, it makes Him a liar, and that's all Satan needs to take His throne. It must accomplish the thing for which it was sent. The only thing that stands in the way of the Word doing its job is us. If we doubt, God is under no obligation to perform.

The written Word of God in the Greek is called, Logos, and for the spoken Word it is called, Rhema. If God has given you a Rhema Word, treat it like a valuable treasure. To the Father, it is every bit as important as His Logos, and it may be even more important, because it was a personal Word that He spoke to you, about you, and just for your situation. You would be wise to stand in faith on that Rhema Word, no matter what the opposition. To do otherwise, is nothing short of blasphemy. Anything less than complete faith in a Word that the Father has spoken to you is doubt.

> ***A man who doubts God is double-minded and will receive nothing from God.*** James 1:8

One day, as I was writing my book called, "Code of Silence," about the power of the spoken Word, I had a mini vision regarding the Kingdom of God, a kind of a modern day parable, if you will. A man was sitting at his breakfast table looking out at his beautifully landscaped yard. It was layered with gorgeous flowers, perfectly manicured bushes, and strategically placed trees. However, due to a recent vacation, weeds had grown up all throughout the entire yard. He realized if he tried to pull the weeds they would just break off, leaving the root and they would grow back again in a few days. He decided to use Round-Up, a chemical weed killer that, when sprayed on the weed, kills the root. He knows that the only way to kill the weed, is to kill the root.

After applying the Round-Up, he goes in the house, makes a sandwich, and sits at his table overlooking his yard, and this is where the problem begins. In his heart, he knows he sprayed the Round-Up, but he's looking at all those weeds and his beautiful yard and it's really driving him nuts. He desperately wants to pull the weeds, because he cannot stand looking at them, but if he does, they will only grow back. This is exactly how it works with us in the Kingdom of God. Once we sow the Word over our situation, we must patiently wait for that word to kill the root of the problem, before we will see the manifestation of the Word that we sowed. The Kingdom of God requires patience.

Remember, like the farmer, find the Word that speaks to your heart, confess it as "Your Word," and stand in faith until it comes to pass, regardless of how long it takes. The following is just a small list, an example of God's Words that children of God can use in times of trouble:

For You have magnified Your Word above Your name. In the day when I cried out, You answered me, and made me bold with strength in my soul. Though I walk in the midst of trouble, You will revive me. Your right hand will save me. Psalm 138:2-7

The LORD redeems the soul of His servants, And none of those who trust in Him shall be found guilty. Ps. 34:22

If anyone conspires against you, it is not of My doing, whosoever would conspire against you shall fall for your sakes. Isaiah 54:15

The Lord will cease that which concerns me; your mercy and loving kindness, O Lord, endures forever, forget not the works of Your own hand. Psalm 138:8

Casting all our cares, anxieties, worries and concerns (once and for all) upon Him, for He cares for us affectionately, and He cares for us watchfully. 1 Peter 5:6-7

Many are the afflictions of the righteous, But the LORD delivers him out of them all. Psalm 34:19

Being fully satisfied and assured that God was able and mighty to keep his Word and do what He has promised. Romans 4:21

It is better to trust God than to put confidence in man. Psalm 118:8

When the righteous cry for help, the Lord hears and delivers them out of all their distress and troubles. The Lord is close to those who are of a broken heart and saves such as are crushed with sorrow for sin and are humbly and thoroughly penitent. Psalm 34:17

… affliction shall not rise up the second time. Nahum 1:9

The angel of ADONAI, who encamps around those who fear him, delivers them. Psalm 34:7

Now this is the confidence that we have in Him, that if we ask anything according to His will, He hears us. 15 And if we know that He hears us, whatever we ask, we know that we have the petitions that we have asked of Him. 1 John 5:14-15

…for God Himself has said, I will not in any way fail you nor give you up nor leave you without support. I will not, I will not, I will not in any degree leave you helpless nor forsake you, nor let you down, or relax my hold on you! Assuredly Not! Hebrews 13:5 (Josh 1:5)

Therefore all those who devour you shall be devoured; And all your adversaries, every one of them, shall go into captivity; Those who plunder you shall become plunder, And all who prey upon you I will make a prey. For I will restore health to you And heal you of your wounds, says the LORD. Jeremiah 30:16-17

So I will restore to you the years that the swarming locust has eaten, The crawling locust, The consuming locust, And the chewing locust. Joel 2:25

Return to the stronghold, You prisoners of hope. Even today I declare that I will restore double to you.
Zech 9:12

I like this next one, because whatever it was that David was dealing with, he must have brought it on himself. He is humbling his heart and seeking the Lord for restoration. Who among us has not been there at one time or another?

O LORD, do not rebuke me in Your wrath, Nor chasten me in Your hot displeasure! For Your arrows pierce me deeply, And Your hand presses me down. There is no soundness in my flesh because of Your anger, Nor any health in my bones because of my sin. For my iniquities have gone over my head; Like a heavy burden they are too heavy for me. My wounds are foul and festering because of my foolishness. I am troubled, I am bowed down greatly; I go mourning all the day long. For my loins are full of inflammation, And there is no soundness in my flesh. I am feeble and severely broken; I groan, because of the turmoil of my heart. Lord, all my desire is before You; And my sighing is not hidden from You. My heart pants, my strength fails me; As for the light of my eyes, it also has gone from me. My loved ones and my friends stand aloof from my plague, And my relatives stand afar off. Those also who seek my life lay snares for me; Those who seek my hurt speak of destruction, And plan deception all the day long. But I, like a deaf man, do not hear; And I am like a mute who does not open his mouth. Thus I am like a man who does not hear, And in whose mouth is no response. For in You, O LORD, I hope; You will hear, O Lord my God. For I said, "Hear me, lest they rejoice over me, Lest, when my foot slips, they exalt themselves against me." For I am ready to fall, And my sorrow is continually before me. For I will declare my iniquity; I will be in anguish over my sin. But my enemies are vigorous, and they are strong; And those who hate me wrongfully have multiplied. Those also who render evil for good, They are my adversaries, because I follow what is good. Do not forsake me, O LORD; O my God, be not far from me! Make haste to help me, O Lord, my salvation!   Psalm 38

Attitude is Everything

As in my own case, the very trial that so heavily weighed me down, the thing that was devastating me was the very thing the Lord used to bring me back to the place where he could use me for The Altar of Love. I had been in the ministry so long that I had grown weary, complacent and other things became more important to me than Jesus.

Life happened, weeds had entered in and the Word that was in me was being choked. Satan used that opportunity to try to destroy me, but God used it to bring me back home. All through Revelation 2 and 3, Jesus is telling the churches to come back to their first love... or else. You cannot come back to something unless you were there at one time, so these churches had loved the Lord at some point.

I look at it like this... where else was I going to go? Who else loves me enough to want what's best for me? Regardless of how my situation works out, who else has my best interest at heart besides Jesus? I just kept hearing Him say, *Trust Me. When are you going to trust Me?* My answer was, "Now and forever more."

Chapter Seven

Love: Leg 4 of The Altar of Love

Jesus said, *Love everybody, as I have loved you, you must love everybody.* Love is not a suggestion... it is a commandment.

If you love Me, you will keep My Commandments. John 14:15

Yes, Jesus has redeemed you from the curse of the Law of Moses, the 613 Levitical laws, but the law of Moses and the Ten Commandments are not the same thing. Jesus has fulfilled the Law of Moses, but we are still expected to obey His Ten Royal Commandments, otherwise, He would not have said so. Satan has deceived the church into thinking that Moses' Law and the Ten Commandments are synonymous, but they are not. Did He not say, *Why do you call me Lord, but do not do what I say?*

He is clearly speaking about His Commandments.

The people honor me with their lips, but their heart is far from me. Because they are ruled by the desires of their flesh and they do not obey my commandments. Matthew 15:8

When we do not obey the Ten Commandments, our hearts are far from Him. To say that our hearts are far from Him, is to say that we don't love Him, and the proof that we don't love Him is the fact that we are not keeping the Commandments.

The opposite of love is not hate. It is selfishness. Satan was selfish. It always had to be about him. In order to love like Jesus loves, you must die to yourself.

For whoever wants to save his life will lose it, but whoever loses his life for My sake will find it. Matthew 16:25

Losing your life to find Jesus is how you die to yourself. Dying to yourself is the only way possible to learn to walk in love, therefore, to walk in love you must first die to yourself.

The concept of, "dying to one's self," is found throughout the New Testament. Truly, it is the essence of the Christian life, in which, we take up our cross and follow Jesus. The principle of, "Dying to one's self," is a central part of being a born again believer; the old self dies and the new man in Christ is born. It is the ultimate walk of love. Jesus spoke repeatedly to His disciples about taking up their cross, which was basically an instrument of death, and following Him. He made it clear that if they wanted to follow Him, they must deny themselves, which means, giving up their lives for Him, spiritually, symbolically, and even, physically, if necessary.

Jesus taught this principle as a requirement, not an option. He was not giving them an A or B choice:

A. Keep their old way of life, their old habits and follow Him, or

B. Deny themselves and Follow Him

No, dying to one's self is a prerequisite for being a follower of Christ. Jesus said that saving your earthly lives would result in losing your soul, but those who willingly give up their lives for His sake would find eternal life.

Then Jesus told his disciples, If anyone would come after me, let him deny himself and take up his cross and follow me. Matthew 16:24–25

Just in case we miss His point here, He puts it another way when He says that those who are unwilling to 'Die to themselves' and live for Him <u>cannot</u> be His disciples,

> *Whoever does not bear his own cross and come after me*
> *cannot be my disciple.* Luke 14:27

Obviously, baptism is not a requirement for salvation, and if it is not, what is the main reason for it? The rite of baptism expresses the commitment of a believer to die to the old, sinful way of life and be reborn to a new life in Christ. Jesus knew that we would have a difficult time grasping this concept of complete surrender and the ritual of baptism. The action of being immersed in the water symbolizes dying and being buried with Christ. This symbolism is precisely why backsliders feel a burning desire to get re-baptized, thereby, rededicating themselves to Jesus and killing off the former lusts of their flesh.

We, therefore, were buried with Him through baptism into death, in order that, just as Christ was raised from the dead through the glory of the Father, we, too, may walk in newness of life. For if we have been united with Him like this in His death, we will certainly, also, be raised to life as He was. We know that our old self was crucified with Him so that the body of sin might be rendered powerless, that we should no longer be slaves to sin. Romans 6:4-8

Likewise, the action of coming out of the water pictures Christ's resurrection. Therefore, much in the same way a parable tells a story to express a spiritual truth in an easy-to-understand way, so too, does baptism portray and identify us with Christ in His death and resurrection. It is a symbol of the life of the Christian that we learn to die to one's self and live for Him who died for us. We learn to live as He lived, walk as He walked, and love as He loves.

In Galatians 2:20 Paul explains this process of dying to one's self, but he uses the phrase 'crucified with Christ,' Saying, *Now, I no longer live, but Christ lives in me.* By Paul's own words, *Now, I no longer live,* He's saying that he is dead, right? I mean, if he no longer lives, the logical conclusion is that he is dead. But he's clearly not dead, so what is he? Dead to himself! Paul's old life, with its propensity to sin and to follow the ways of the world, is now dead, and the new Paul is the dwelling place of Christ, who lives in and through him.

Paul, who gladly gave his body as a vessel, totally sold out to Jesus. Jesus uses His adopted children to love the lost and dying of this world, because He's not here to do it any longer, but it's still in His heart to do. His heart hasn't changed since He ascended. He still loves His creation, and while He is not here to do it Himself, He has millions of co-heirs to love through. That's our job, to allow ourselves to be used by Jesus to love everybody.

So, how does one learn to die to oneself? Is it really even possible? It sounds nearly impossible. Can people really learn to die to themselves, especially in this modern, false grace, do-whatever-pleases-you society, where everything is focused around you? Yes, and it's easier than you think. The ability to truly die to one's self hangs on one profound, yet simple commandment... love.

A new Commandment I give you: Love everybody, as I have loved you, love everybody. John 13:34

Love the Lord your God with all your heart and with all your soul and with all your mind. This is the first and greatest commandment. And the second is like it: *Love your neighbor as yourself. On these two commandments hang all the Law and the Prophets.* Matthew 22:37-39

If you're thinking to yourself, That's so much easier than having to keep the Ten Commandments, now I only have two. If you think that, you are fooling yourself. This new Commandment of love is much more encompassing than the original ten ever were. Before Jesus, you were only guilty of sinning if you physically broke the Commandment. In other words, a man was only guilty of adultery if he had sex with a woman other than his wife, but Jesus said,

But I tell you that anyone who looks at a woman to lust after her has already committed adultery with her in his heart. Matthew 5:28

Before you go freaking out, thinking there is no way for you to do it, remember, that God has given us the blessing of repentance and confession. That's right, repentance and confession is a blessing, and be grateful we are in an era that we still have this benefit. There will come a day when the opportunity to repent and confess will no longer present itself. I advise you, take advantage of it now and repent and confess daily, because everyone sins.

So, how is love the key to dying to one's self? Simple, love takes the focus off of you and puts it on everyone, but you. It is the selfish, self-centered attitude that makes dying to oneself seem like an impossibility, but the true essence of love shifts the focus off of you and puts it on people other than yourself. As I said before, the opposite of love is not hate, but selfishness, and the inability to die to one's self is a spirit of selfishness.

When you shift the focus from you and put it on the people that God has put in your life, you begin to crucify your own desires and put the needs of others ahead of you. We have to come to the realization that the world does not revolve around us. We are to become selfless, and when we finally come to terms with that, when we finally understand that our focus is not on getting blessed, on me, my four and no more, but on becoming a blessing for the lost and dying, then and only then can we die to ourselves and learn to love like Jesus. This concept of selfless love is a contradiction to the prosperity gospel, whose main message is on getting blessed rather than being a blessing. Sure, they are encouraged to give, but only because they want to receive. They desire a return on their giving like an investment. True love gives, expecting nothing in return. Therefore, if the prosperity gospel is the opposite of love, then it is not from Jesus, and if it's not, we know then whom it is from.

Now, this principle of dying to one's self is in direct opposition to the new hyper grace, "once saved always saved" (OSAS) doctrine of the Masonic Christian preachers in their mega churches. That's right, you heard me correctly, I am calling them what I heard the Lord call them. Several months ago, I was preparing for church, when I clearly heard the Holy Spirit tell me that the prosperity message and the OSAS message, which go hand-in-hand, was a deception of Masons who had infiltrated the church to "fleece the sheep." It is designed to rob the Children of God blind, and lead them into sin and ultimately to Hell through selfishness, greed, and disobedience.

You won't find a "die to one's self" teaching in a mega grace, OSAS church. It simply does not fit the hidden narrative of, "Do what pleases you. You're saved. What's the difference?" It is a selfish, self-centered attitude and the complete opposite of the message of love that Jesus taught and displayed. Jesus desperately needs us to understand and walk out this kind of love, so He can love His creation through us. As adopted children and co-heirs with Christ, our goal should not be to get a blessing, but to give or be a blessing. Then, and only then, will we be in a place where He can finally use us the way He desires, to love others.

Dying to self does not mean we lose our personalities or become insensible, rather, 'dying to self,' means that the old you, your old way of thinking and your old life are put to death. Mainly, the sinful ways and lifestyles we once engaged in are expected to die, so that Christ may live in us.

> *Those who belong to Christ Jesus have crucified the sinful nature with its passions and desires.* Galatians 5:24

Where we once pursued selfish pleasures, we now pursue love with equal passion, because that's what pleases God. In Scripture, 'dying to one's self' is never portrayed as something we choose to do or not do. It's not an option. It is a commandment for everyone who considers themselves a Christian. Jesus didn't say, "Hey guys, if you're thinking of following me, you should really consider taking up your cross." That's an absurd teaching, but a very real and popular one nowadays. Dying to one's self is the evidence of the new birth, the "fruit," if you will.

> *Beware of false prophets, who come to you in sheep's*

clothing, but inwardly they are ravenous wolves. You will know them by their fruits… Every tree that does not bear good fruit is cut down and thrown into the fire. Therefore, by their fruits you will know them. Matthew 7:15-20

Clearly, Jesus is saying that fruit is the outward manifestation of the spirit within us. Good fruit = Spirit of God = Love. Bad fruit = spirit of the world = selfishness. The phrase, "You will know them," is referring to their allegiance. They are either loyal to the Lord God or to the Devil and the evidence of their loyalty is their fruit. Fruit, is the way in which we conduct ourselves, our walk of Love, our ability to die to ourselves, or live for the world.

And what jumped out at me was verse 19, in which, Jesus said, *Every tree that does not bear good fruit is cut down and thrown into the fire.* It does not take a rocket scientist to understand what He is saying. If we do not figure this love thing out, if we do not learn to walk in love, if we do not crucify our flesh and die to ourselves, Jesus is saying that we risk the very real possibility of Hell. Now, don't get mad at me, I didn't say it. If you don't like the saying, take it up with Jesus.

No one can come to Jesus unless he is willing to see his old life crucified and begin to live in obedience to Him. In Revelation 3, Jesus describes the believers who are unwilling to crucify their flesh as lukewarm followers, who try to live partly in the old life and partly in the new. It's His description of what He will do with them that is most alarming.

So, because you are lukewarm, and neither hot nor cold, I am going to vomit you out of My mouth. Revelation 3:15–16

That lukewarm condition characterized the church of Laodicea, as well as, most OSAS, prosperity preachers today. Being "lukewarm" is nothing more than rebellion, and rebellion is the epitome of selfishness and the opposite of Love. In most translations, the term "spit out" means "to vomit out," but if you look at the Greek word "emeo" (em-eh'-o), it means "to reject with extreme disgust." It's like the time you got so sick and your body desperately needed to rid itself of whatever it was that was poisoning it and it comes out in a fashion referred to as projectile vomiting.

The underlying character of the OSAS, false grace doctrine is an unwillingness to die to one's self and live for Christ. It is nothing more than a well laid snare of the enemy for most people who consider themselves Christians, but never really come to the understanding of how to submit and obey. These people understand that Satan is real and are smart enough to determine that they do not want to go to hell. They gravitate to the OSAS, feel good, mega churches, because they never teach the danger of sin for fear of losing tithes.

These lukewarm Christians never learn that scripture says their rebellion is as the sin of witchcraft and a direct acquiescence to Satan's will and number one motto, "Do what thou wilt." Their unwillingness to submit, obey and die to one's self is a rebellious spirit. It's the same rebellious attitude that got Satan kicked out of Heaven and proves that the OSAS doctrine is directly from Satan himself, because it's right out of his playbook. The OSAS doctrine and dying to one's self are diametrically opposed to one another. Dying to one's self is not an option for Christians. It's a choice that leads to eternal life.

Let's look at this from another angle, beginning with what Jesus didn't mean. Many people interpret the cross as some burden they must carry in their lives: a strained relationship, a thankless job, a physical illness. With self-pitying pride, they have this attitude of, "That's just my cross, the burden I am destined to carry in life." But that's not what Jesus meant when He said, *Take up your cross and follow Me.*

When Jesus carried His cross to Golgotha to be crucified, no one was thinking it was symbolic of the burden He would carry. No, to a person in the first-century, the cross meant one thing and one thing only, death by the most painful and humiliating means human beings could conceive. Today, modern Christians view the cross as a cherished symbol of atonement, forgiveness, grace, and love. But in Jesus' day, the cross represented a horrible, torturous death. The Romans forced convicted criminals to carry their own crosses to the place of crucifixion. Bearing a cross meant to carry your own execution device, while facing ridicule along the way.

Therefore, *Take up your cross and follow Me,* means being willing to die to yourself in order to allow Jesus to love other people through you. It's a call to absolute surrender. As well, whenever Jesus commanded them to bare their cross, He followed it up with the consequences of what would happen if they did not.

For whoever tries to save his life will lose it, but whoever loses his life for my sake will save it. For what does it profit a man to gain the whole world but destroy his soul or lose it? Luke 9:24-25

Look, I know this is a big pill to swallow, but walking in love is not an option for us. It is a Commandment. It is a hard saying

166

and one the enemy will use against its teaching, with words like "legalism" and "faith by works," but remember, I didn't say it, Jesus did. And while it may be a tough one to come to terms with, the reward is Heaven. Trust me, there isn't a soul in Hell that wouldn't gladly switch places with you for just one more chance to die to themselves and walk in love.

The Christian life is easy when it runs smoothly, but our true commitment to Him is revealed during trials. Trials separate the mature believer from the posers and the hypocrites. Jesus warned us that trials would come.

I have said these things to you, that in me you may have peace. In the world you will have tribulation. But be of good cheer; I have overcome the world. John 16:33

Discipleship demands sacrifice, and Jesus never hid that cost.

Follow me. But the disciple said, Lord, let me first go and bury my father. And Jesus said to him, Let the dead to bury the dead. But as for you, go and proclaim the Kingdom of God. Another said, I will follow you, Lord, but let me first say farewell to those at my home. Jesus said to him, No one who puts his hand to the plow and looks back is fit for the Kingdom of God. Matthew 8:21

My favorite example of a failure to die to one's self is found in a parable that Jesus tells in Luke 14,

A certain man prepared a great banquet and invited many guests. When it was time for the banquet, he sent his servant to tell those who had been invited, Come, for everything is now ready. But one after another, they all began to make excuses. The first one said, I have bought a field and I need to go see it. Please excuse me. Another said, I have bought five yoke of oxen and I am going to try them out. Please excuse me. Still another said, I married a wife, so I can't come. Luke 14:16-20

They all seemed willing to follow Jesus, but when it came time to put up or shut up, all they had were excuses. They failed to account for the cost of not following Him. None was willing to take up his cross and crucify their own interests.

On multiple occasions, Jesus appears to almost dissuade His followers by telling them the truth of what was going to happen to them if they followed Him.

If the world hates you, know that it has hated me before it hated you. If you were of the world, the world would love you as its own; but because you are not of the world, but I chose you out of the world, therefore the world hates you. Remember the word that I said to you: A servant is not greater than his master. If they persecuted me, they will also persecute you. If they kept my word, they will also keep yours. But all these things they will do to you on account of my name, because they do not know Him who sent me. If I had not come and spoken to them, they would not have been guilty of sin, but now they have no excuse for their sin. Whoever hates me hates my Father also. If I had not done among them the works that no one else did, they would not be guilty of sin, but now they have seen and hated both me and my Father. But the word that is written in their Law must be fulfilled: They hated me without a cause... I have said all these things to you to keep you from falling away. They will put you out of the synagogues. Indeed, the hour is coming when whoever kills you will think he is offering service to God. And they will do

these things, because they have not known the Father, nor me.
But I have said these things to you, that when their hour
comes you may remember that I told them to you.
John 15:18-16:4

It almost sounds as if Jesus was trying to talk them out of
following Him with His honesty. That's not exactly the best way
to recruit people, by telling them they will suffer and die
terrible deaths. Although, if you think about it, it needed to be
done. If He could talk them out of following Him by simply
telling them the truth during the good times, then they would
have never lasted through the tough times.

If you think that's bad, listen to Paul describe what he had to
endure in 2 Corinthians,

I have worked harder, been put in prison more often, been
whipped times without number, and faced death again and
again. Five different times the Jewish leaders gave me thirty-
nine lashes. Three times I was beaten with rods. Once I was
stoned. Three times I was shipwrecked. Once I spent a whole
night and a day adrift at sea. I have traveled on many long
journeys. I have faced danger from rivers and from robbers. I
have faced danger from my own people, the Jews, as well as
from the Gentiles. I have faced danger in the cities, in the
deserts, and on the seas. And I have faced danger from men
who claim to be believers but are not. I have worked hard and
long, enduring many sleepless nights. I have been hungry and
thirsty and have often gone without food. I have shivered in
the cold, without enough clothing to keep me warm.
2 Cor. 11:23-27

How different is what Paul experienced from the modern day Gospel presentation sold to us by the OSAS prosperity peddlers! How many people would respond to an altar call that went something like this, "Come follow Jesus. For if you do, you will likely lose your oldest and dearest friends, get shunned by your closest family members, soil your reputation, lose your career, and possibly even your life? Likely, you will be hated, many of you will lose everything and become broke, some of you will even become homeless, you'll be beaten, spit on, imprisoned and maybe even killed!" How many people would respond to that a call? I'll bet the number of false converts would likely decrease dramatically!

For God so loved the world that He gave His only begotten son. Love is a giving attitude, not a taking one. When you love, you prefer another over yourself. Loving them means you give them the last drink, you give them the last piece of food, you give the best seat. Love gives. Selfishness takes. Love does not have to get even, it is not spiteful, it doesn't need to have the last word or win the argument. Love is gentle, submissive, trusting, faithful, positive, helpful, caring, and considerate.

Learn to be patient with others that are not where you are spiritually, for you, too, were once lost until you were found. Be patient with yourself for although you may fall at times, Jesus will be there to pick you up. Be patient in the midst of trials, because they always serve as an opportunity for the Father to work a miracle in and through you. As it is written, you overcome by the blood of the lamb and the word of your testimony. How can you have a testimony without a test?

Faith is like a muscle, if it is not exercised, it will atrophy. How can one exercise his faith without a trial? Therefore, do not begrudge your trials for their intended purpose is to develop your faith and character. Love is kind. Whoever heard of a mean Christian? If you tell someone you don't care, you are saying you don't love, and if you don't love, you are not a Christian. If they are a human, we're supposed to care. Love is not jealous or envious. If Jesus decides to bless someone, what business is it of yours? Be glad for those around you whom the Lord decides to bless. Your bad attitude may be the very reason you are not walking in the same blessings. Learn to trust Him. Be not like your Father's enemy. For love does not brag, it is not prideful, or arrogant. Remember that pride comes before the fall.

God opposes the proud, but gives grace to the humble. Jas 4:6

Love is never rude, does not anger easily, and never, ever keeps account of wrongs done unto you. Likewise, when you forgive, never use it against that person again. You must treat them like your Father does you. When your Father forgives you, it goes into a sea of forgetfulness. Do not throw it back in their face. If you do, you never really forgave them.

Love always looks for the good in people. You are to be a gold miner, not a dirt digger. Jesus hates gossip and love does not talk about people behind their back. If you would not say it to their face, you shouldn't say it at all. Love never gives up on people, no matter how many times they disappoint you. Never give up on yourself, no matter how many times you fall. Get up and forge ahead. In Hebrews 13:5, Paul quotes God himself saying, *I will never under any circumstances, desert you, nor give you up, nor leave you without support, nor will I, in any degree leave you helpless, nor will I forsake or let you down or relax My hold on you... assuredly not!* Like I always say... where else can you go? Love never loses faith. He will never leave you, nor forsake you.

Love is not arrogant or rude to others regardless of whether they are right or wrong. Love is not irritable and does not wake up on the wrong side of the bed. If you wake up in a bad mood, you are just plain selfish. You have just made the day about you. Doing so is intimidating and manipulating people to cater to your bad mood, and both intimidation and manipulation are forms of witchcraft. If you have behaved like this in the past, repent.

Love is not easily provoked, it will not allow itself to be baited into an argument, and it keeps no record of when it has been wronged. Love does not have to get even. Love is not glad in injustice, it is not happy when evil happens to others, even if it seems well deserved. Love rejoices when the truth prevails (that which God says about a situation). Love stands firm even in seemingly impossible situations. Love never loses faith and never gives up hope. Love endures to the end, regardless of how long it may take. Love always wins in the end. Love conquers all.

Love thinks no evil. Thinks - logizomai (log-id'-zom-ahee); NT:3049 to take an inventory, to conclude, reason, reckon, suppose, think-on. Evil - kakos (kak-os'); NT:2556 depraved, or injurious: bad, evil, harm, wicked.

There is an old saying, "If you don't have anything nice to say, don't say anything at all." This commandment of 'love thinks no evil,' goes one step further than telling us that we are not supposed to say anything bad, but we are not supposed to even think badly about another. Love demands that we give people the benefit of the doubt. It means that love, or that a person under the influence of love, is not malicious, not looking to find fault, or to impute improper motives to others. A person walking in love should not automatically think there was any evil intention, even in cases which might tend to be repetitive or obvious. Love is the desire to think well of people, their motives, opinions, and conduct until we are compelled, otherwise, by the most unbreakable evidence.

Everything the father has is yours if you learn to walk in love and serve Him, but you are never under obligation to do so. It must be done out of love for Jesus. Not for personal gain or prestige, but with a humble, grateful heart. Understand, this is not a sprint, it is a marathon.

Do not grow weary in doing good, for in due time you will reap a harvest, if you do not give up. Galatians 6:9

If you sow words of love and compassion, love and compassion will return to you. If, however, out of bitter envy and selfish pursuit, you sow insults, strife and divisions, the same shall return to you.

Do not be deceived: God is not mocked, for whatever one sows, that will he also reap. Galatians 6:7

Do unto others as you would have do unto you. Jesus said, *Love everybody, as I have loved you. No greater love has any man than to lay down his life for his friends.* Jesus gave His life for you. If you want eternal life, you must give your life to Him. This is the deal He offers, and it's your choice to accept it or not. He has prepared us for this very purpose and given us his spirit as a guarantee, if we believe in what He says and are faithful to do it.

Love is patient, (in trials, with self, with others)

Love is kind/say something positive or don't say anything at all

Love is not jealous or envious of others

Love does not brag / don't think too highly of yourself

Love is not arrogant / pride comes directly from Satan

Love is not rude / whoever heard of a rude Christian

Love is not selfish / God so loved us that He Gave Jesus. Loves Gives

Love is not easily angered / if needed, put yourself in a time out

Love keeps no account of wrongs - God will not throw your sins back in your face and neither should we. Forgive and forget.

Love never gives up – Don't give up on people no matter how many times they fall. Remember, that we, too, were once in that same state. Don't give up on yourself, sometimes it's a process. Besides, where else can you go? You certainly can't go back to the world. They will kill you, now that you have changed teams.

Love never loses faith - Who else can save you?

Love is always hopeful – always look for the best in people, be a gold miner not dirt digger!

Chapter Eight

5 Things that will Give Up Your Superpower... Your Authority

I. If you do nothing. Authority is there to be assumed. If you do not assume it, then Satan will.

II. Practicing Sin. Jesus said, Go away you workers of iniquity. It implies someone who knows his behavior is sinful, but does it anyway, dismissing it as being covered by grace. It, also, implies continual or habitual sin. As with all sin, be quick to repent and ask forgiveness. Sinful behavior to stay away from: Everything and anything associated with the occult, lying, cheating, stealing, lust, drunkenness, revelries, drugs, vulgarity, whoredom, harlotries, fornication, adultery, gossip, manipulation, intimidation, and rebellion.

III. Words. The power (Authority) the Devil has is the power (Authority) we give him by the words we speak. Death and life are in the power (Authority) of your tongue. Take no thought repeating what the Devil is whispering in your ear.

IV. Walking outside Love. When we allow ourselves to act or react outside of love, we give up our Authority. Feelings and emotions that can give away your Authority: Anger, rage, resentment, bitterness, contentions, selfishness, haughtiness, arrogance, pride, indigence, envy, strife, jealousy, unforgiveness, and greed.

V. Witchcraft of the Heart, also referred to in scripture as Works of the Flesh. This happens at all levels of Christianity, from baby Christians to mature believers. One expects these behaviors to be only in baby Christians, so when they exist in a mature believer, there had to be a breakdown somewhere in their walk of faith or lack, thereof. It could be they rebelled and rejected correction, maybe they were not fortunate to have good Bible-based instruction as they developed, or maybe they just neglected to continually till the soil of their heart. Regardless, the Devil has sown weeds in the form of demonic behaviors like rebellion, seduction, arrogance, lust, bitterness, quarreling, drunkenness, carousing, self seeking etc. Satan will use these people like pawns to bring division and offense into the body of Christ. I highly advise that you go through the list circumspectly and see if you fit any one of these behaviors. Many times they are generational and passed down from family member to family member. If you notice one or more of these in your personality, repent, ask forgiveness and cast that thing to the pit of Hell, never to return.

A complete list of witchcraft of the heart is provided in the following Chapter, Occult Activities.

Chapter Nine

Occult Activities

Let no one be found among you who sacrifices his son or daughter in the fire, who practices divination or sorcery, interprets omens, engages in witchcraft, or casts spells, or who is a medium or spiritualists or who consults the dead. Anyone who does these things is detestable to the Lord, and because of these detestable practices the Lord your God will drive out those nations before you. You must be blameless before the Lord your God. Deuteronomy 18:10-13

God hates occult practice. To do so is like committing adultery on God. Through it, you are worshiping His mortal enemy. You are basically saying that God's way is not good enough for you, that you are going to go over to this Satan fella and try it His way. That is just a big slap in the face of your Father, and I highly warn you against it.

Way too many people either have, or are engaging in, all sorts of occult practices such as divination, astrology, voodoo, witchcraft, and the like. They search for answers to life's challenges: seeking riches, power, and vengeance. Many others sought the occult as a means by which to accomplish goals via manipulating people with spells and hexes. The main problem with participating in occult practices is that it is ultimately designed to kill you. Practitioners of the occult open themselves and their family's lives to demonic activity, demonic possession, and oppression. Occult practices such as ouija boards, tarot cards, contacting the dead, palm reading, fortune telling, divination, etc., are to be avoided by Christians and the non-Christians, alike.

What is Occult?

The word Occult is a Latin word which means, hidden, secret or mysterious. Therefore, one could define 'occult' as using secret, hidden supernatural knowledge and practices in order to achieve an objective. The definition of occult is: of or pertaining to magic, astrology or any system claiming use or knowledge of secret or supernatural powers or agencies.

The first thing the Holy Spirit began teaching me regarding The Altar of Love was to focus on removing all demonic spirits attached to people by way of the occult activity they engaged in during their lifetime. It started the day after I got the vision of The Altar of Love. I was still in the process of writing the vision and the word I received as it was given by the Holy Spirit, so I wasn't all the way there yet, not even close.

I was sitting on the outside isle in church that Sunday and I felt a tap on my shoulder. It was one of the elders asking if I would help the young lady she was escorting. I looked at the woman, then I looked back at the elder and she was making crazy eyes at me from behind the woman, as not to be seen. You know that look people make behind the back of another to indicate something is not right? That's the look she was giving me. Then she said, "She's dealing with some demonic strongholds that are way beyond me and I thought you might be able to help."

I thought, sure, why not, on the job training. "Gladly," I said, and I proceeded to escort her out of the service. We walked over to a nearby stairwell and we sat down side-by- side on the second step. I asked her to tell me what she was dealing with and she responded with a litany of things that I would have needed to write down to remember. Later I learned to do just that. She was addicted to drugs and alcohol and had been for years. She was in and out of trouble, and always making bad decisions. She said that she knew God, but like so many others, she had dabbled in the occult. She had multiple ailments, sicknesses, and diseases and her symptoms kept her in constant, severe back pain. She had bad knees, as well as, pain in her neck and shoulders. She was a mess.

The first thing I did was tell her I loved her. She was not made up very well, a bit over weight, and I could tell that her self-esteem was in the tank. She looked at me in shock when I said it, and I assure you I was not patronizing her when I did. I genuinely loved her. It was remarkable. It's like I could feel the love Jesus has for us, coming through me to her. I asked her if she knew who she was and she told me her name. I smiled at her and asked if she was a believer and she said that she was saved as a little girl. I questioned her about salvation and what she thought it was and how it worked. I was satisfied she had a good understanding of what it meant to be saved.

This was imperative, because if she does not understand salvation, I cannot proceed with evicting the demonic spirits, until she does. Otherwise, all those spirits will return, as soon as, I leave the room and she will be worse off than before. I took her arm and wrapped it in mine and I began to tell her who she was. I began to tell her about her Identity, that she was a Child of God, and an heir to the throne. I told her what it meant to be an heir, and how she stands to inherit everything her Father has, which is everything. I described it to her as if she was the daughter of Bill Gates and all the while I'm looking at her carefully.

I'm looking to see a glimmer of hope. I'm looking to see the light bulb go on. I'm looking for the moment she gets what I'm trying to tell her, so I can move on, because you cannot go to Authority until they fully understand their Identity. I tell her how she was adopted and that she is seated in Heavenly places with Christ Jesus, far above all principalities and demonic powers. I tell her that she is a daughter of the King and He wants her to know who she is, then I see it. I see the light go on and she smiles really big, so I ask her, "Who are you?" and with a huge smile she says, "I'm a daughter of the King. I'm a Child of God," and I know, right there, I got her. She's going to be free today.

Next, I begin to tell her about her Authority, about how she was created to have dominion over the works of God's hands. That everything the Father has made was made for her to rule over. I explained the meaning of Authority, how it made her the sheriff, with the badge, the gun, the court, and the jail. I told her that she was the judge, jury and executioner and she began to smile even bigger. I told her about what Jesus said about giving her Authority to trample on serpents and scorpions. I told her that to trample on something meant that she was master over it, that she dominated it. I told her that serpents and scorpions were just metaphors for Satan and the demon forces. I told her that Jesus said her Authority was over all the power of the enemy and nothing could hurt her. I explained to her that Jesus never lied or exaggerated, so if nothing could hurt her, then nothing could hurt her, whatsoever. I asked her, "If nothing can hurt you, what do you have to be afraid of?" "Nothing," she said. Then, I looked into her eyes and now she's got Authority. I know she got it, because her smile disappeared and she got angry, and that was exactly what I was looking for. You see, there is such a thing as righteous indignation and this was it. She said, "You mean to tell me that all this time I've had the Authority, but I let him do this to me?" "Yep. Are you ready to take your Authority back and evict those foul buggers?" I asked. "Oh Hell yeah!" she said enthusiastically. From there I had her go through all the things she had done in the occult. Even though she was a believer, she still had played with ouija boards, palm readings, psychic hotlines, etc. She was very active sexually, as well, so we spent considerable time repenting and asking forgiveness for all her occult practices, as well as, her past sins. When we finished, I asked her how she felt and she said, "I feel nauseous," "Good," I said, "Now let's make them go." Later, I would revise the process a bit, but it works just as well, either way.

I began speaking to the demonic spirits that had attached to her when she played with the ouija board and I commanded them to go, in the name of Jesus. With that, she let out a large belch. Embarrassed, she covered her mouth and apologized. I laughed and told her it was quite normal and to expect much more of the same. And there was. For the next 20 minutes, she belched and belched and belched until there were no more demons left to belch.

When we were done, I asked her how she felt and she smiled the biggest smile and said, "Free. For the first time in years, I feel free...and light. I feel 100 pounds lighter." I said, "Now let's test out the healing, get up." She stood and began walking around. I asked her if she could touch her toes and she said that she could not. Her back was so messed up, she hadn't bent over in years. I said, "Do it now." She bent over and put her hands flat on the ground, stood up and freaked out.

She's crying now and gives me a big hug, and I say, "Just hold up now, we're not done. Didn't you say that you had arthritis really bad in your knees?" "Oh yeah," she said. I said, "When was the last time you did a squat?" "Not for 10 years," she said. I told her to squat and she goes right to the floor, like it's nothing. Now, she's really excited, because these are things that she has been dealing with for over a decade and now they are completely gone. After a few more minutes of this, we realized she is completely healed, from head to toe. Suddenly, she begins weeping as all her emotional baggage is now washing away with her tears. But it was a good cry, a happy cry. After another 10 minutes or so, when I'm fairly certain there was nothing left to evict, we were done.

That was my first Altar of Love case and it was a complete success. I have seen that woman in church since then and she is still pain and addiction free. Since then I added the power of words and the walk of love, but the principle remains the same. Teach people who they are, what their Authority is, how to watch their words, and how to walk in love and no power in Hell can stand against it. It works every time, all the time, unless I miss something, as in the case of the woman, whose mother bought her the ouija board. You cannot skip or rush the process or it will leave holes.

Each time I took a case, I learned something new about how the spirits operate. Once I was confidant with the process, I was doing up to as many as 4 cases per day. Considering that an average case can take upwards of 4 hours, it was consuming an enormous amount of my personal time. I learned that everyone has dabbled with the occult, in one way or another, even when they swear they have not. Some of it is much worse than others. The spirits associated with ouija boards are much more powerful than those associated with horoscopes, but don't let that give you a false sense of assurance, because these spirits, having gained access, will usher in others more wicked than themselves.

While spirits associated with occult practices are expert at the art of mind confusion, depression, schizophrenia and suicide, as well as, other mental and emotional disorders, they are, also, adept at sickness and disease. In the 70's, my mother attended a psychic camp of sorts, where many spiritualists were present offering their services of palm reading, psychic readings, and crystal healing, and such. Upon returning, she was telling a co-worker at her job about the experience. Her co-worker asked her if she had ever read Deuteronomy 28, which talks about the curses that come with such activity. After she read it, she repented and asked forgiveness and never went back, but all her friends did. There was an entire group that went every year and one-by-one they began to die, horrible deaths from strange and incurable diseases. My mother is in her mid-70's and still in very good health, but all of her friends have long since been deceased.

There are many activities that seem innocuous, but are in fact, an opening for demonic spirits and much of it aimed at children. Obviously, the Harry Potter books and movies were a huge advancement for the occult movement. Pokémon and Yu-gi-oh cards are, also, doorways to demons. Dungeons and Dragons, horror movies, and TV networks like Disney and Nickelodeon all act as gateways for demonic spirits. Actually, just about anything Disney puts out has an occult theme to it, nowadays. Even their logo has the 666 in it. If it has witchcraft or sorcery in it, stay away from it. Here is a list of occult activities to avoid. There may be more I am unaware of, but this is a start:

Clairvoyance, letters of protection, mediums, second sight, self-hypnosis, metaphysics, auras, trances, hypnosis, mental science, self-realization, pagan holidays, Jezebel, Ahab, seances, witchcraft, black magic, white magic, fortune-telling, red magic, ruler of witchcraft, neutral or gray magic, palm-reading, baptism of witchcraft, charms, Buddhism, serpent charmers, omens, good luck charms, crystal balls, ouija boards, evil eye, occult fears, levitation, black arts, Devil's foot, conjuration, occult symbols, karma, astrology, birth signs, necromancy, Mormonism, fetishes, amulets, birth stones, spells, incarnations, spirit guides, potions, sorcery, curses, apparitions, ghosts, poltergeists, ESP, kabala, horoscopes, clairvoyance, PK (psychokinesis), voodoo, clairaudience, pass the fire, telepathy, rebellion, stubbornness, meditation, parapsychology, palm-reading, yoga, alchemy, the hearing of noises, Kung-fu, psychic portraits, third eye, yin-yang, crystal ball, pendulums, Catholicism, Hinduism, tarot cards, mediums, spiritualism, metaphysical healing, tea leaves, star-gazing, Satan worship, black mass, numerology, idol worship, prognostication, mental telepathy, multiplied curses, Jehovah Witnesses, calling evil spirits, lust for dominance, female dominance, Christian Science healing, communication with the dead, occult artwork, magic healing through wart or burn charming, anything that predicts your future or advises your life; even some Christian music has occult symbolism woven into it, and Satanic inspired music, which is just about every kind of music with lyrics.

Many of those who had practiced magic brought their books together and burned them in the sight of all. And they counted up the value of them, and it totaled fifty thousand pieces of silver. Acts 19:19

If you have anything in your house that is occult by nature, burn it. If you are not sure of its origin, if you are not sure about the person who gave it to you, if you brought it back as an artifact from another country, burn it. I know it sounds harsh, but if there is even a reasonable doubt, better safe than sorry. If it is of great value, I suppose you can sell it, but I would put a disclaimer on it when you do, so the person buying it is fully aware of what they are buying. I have had this discussion with many of my case subjects that have told me they had already cleaned out their home years ago, but I make them do it again, anyway, and they always come back and tell me they found so much more. Some have found as much as three garbage bags full of stuff. Burn it, burn it, burn it and when in doubt, burn it. If you have old rock and roll albums or CD's, burn them. If you cannot burn things where you are, throw them in a dumpster somewhere, but get them out of your house A.S.A.P!

Going back to the 60's, all the major record companies took the master tape into a room with 12 witches and warlocks, where they conjured spirits into the master, so that every record produced came complete with its very own demon spirit, nice and personal like. Don't think for a second that it is relegated only to this music or that music, because if it's recorded, it is demonically inspired and infused. All the major record companies were run by Satanists, at that time. However, smaller independent ones may not have been. Currently, <u>all</u>

news media, all recording studios, all movie production studios, all TV networks, the fashion industry, the newspaper industry, the banking and investment industry, and even all of the professional sports leagues are run by Luciferians. It's not hard to see. They don't even hide it anymore. In fact, they openly promote it now.

There are more than a few sites devoted to finding demonic symbolism in Christian music, as well, and I can honestly say that their evidence was conclusive. In no way am I saying that all Christian music is demonic, however, we'd be stupid to assume that Satan would not or could not infiltrate the industry. Remember, they have many codes and symbols that they use to communicate with rank and file members, and they are expected to flash their symbols and signs as a gang member throws up his gang signs.

If you have a friend or relative in your family that is a professed witch and dabbles in the occult, take everything they have ever given to you and burn it. Do not take anything from them again and do not let them in your house again. If you have to have a relationship with them, meet them away from your home. Try not to touch them in any way as that is the easiest form of transfer. If there is no way around it and you have to have them over, anoint your house with oil, loose angels round about your home at every doorway, and instruct them to not let any demonic spirits enter your home. Remember, you have the Authority, but you have to use it. Not only is binding and loosing part of your Authority, it is your responsibility. Those warring angels are disappointed when they don't have anything to do. Keep them busy. It's what they love doing.

They were made for this very purpose. In the Complete Jewish Bible, Psalm 34 says,

The angels of ADONAI, who encamps around those who fear him, delivers them. Psalm 34:8

For He will command His angels concerning you to guard you in all your ways. Psalm 91:11

If you have children, never let them be in contact with anyone from the occult. All it takes is one touch to transfer a spirit of homosexuality into a child who is too young to sense the change. Clearly you didn't think that homosexuality was a biological thing. If it were, animals would be homosexual, but they're not. Only humans are, because we contend with these fouls spirits. If a host body is resistant to the spirit and will not acquiesce to its demands, it will look for a more pliable host.

Submit to God, resist the Devil, and he will flee from you. James 4:7

As soon as the spirit finds a new more easily corruptible host, it will make the transfer upon touch. If the host body is dying, the spirit will attempt to make a transfer before the host is deceased.

You shall burn the carved images of their God's with fire; you shall not covet the silver or gold that is on them, nor take it for yourselves, lest you be snared by it; for it is an abomination to the Lord your God. Nor shall you bring an abomination into your house, lest you be doomed to destruction like it; but you shall utterly detest it and utterly abhor it, for it is an accursed thing. Deuteronomy 7:25 & 26

One day, not long ago, I was having lunch with my friend, Miss Ralphena, when I looked at her finger to see a humongous ring in the shape of the All Seeing Eye, except that it was long ways on her finger, so she did not notice it. I asked if she wouldn't mind taking it off and giving it to me for a second. When she did, I turned it sideways, so it looked like the Eye of Horus, that it was intended to be and I showed it to her that way. Her jaw almost hit the table, when she realized she had been wearing the All Seeing Eye of the enemy on her hand.

She told me the story about how she had just finished preaching for a large group of women at a conference and she had begun praying for them. They had pressed in real close to her as she laid hands on them one-by-one. A woman came from nowhere, and put the ring inside her bra. Apparently women do that with each other, because she said she didn't have a problem with it. When she got back to the hotel, she took it out and marveled at the sheer size of the stones. The eye was a 3 or 4 carrot ruby, surrounded by 20, or so, very large diamond baguettes.

I must admit, it was beautiful, but it was equally as evil looking. She had been suffering many serious, life-threatening illnesses all beginning only days after receiving the ring. Then, I had a vision of them actually watching her through the eye of the ring. In case I had not mentioned it earlier, Miss Ralphena specializes in demonic warfare and has been doing it for 30 plus years. She had been wreaking havoc on Satan's kingdom, so it appeared like they wanted to keep tabs on her and kill her in the process. That is why you never take gifts from strangers.

She decided to give it to a jeweler friend of hers, that specializes in creative designs. A few weeks later we met again for lunch and I asked her about it. She said that her friend was having trouble deciding what to do with it and needed some more time. The following month we met again, and again I asked her about it. She said that she asked the jeweler a second time and this time he really went on and on about how he could not do anything with it and that there was something wrong with it that made him feel strange every time he went to work on it. She then proceeded to tell him to destroy it. And that, my friends, is the way you deal with demonic artifacts.

Indicators of Satanic Involvement

It is not 100% proof that someone is involved in Satanism when you find one or two of these things, but it does mean you should look closer. Check their bedroom, and other personal spaces. If you uncover a number of these signs, it is a good indicator that the person is dabbling in the occult.

Look for These Signs:

- Occult drawings on books, notebooks
- Discovery of a diary (called a Book of Shadows) filled with strange signs, symbols, drawings (pentagrams, 666, horned figures etc.), and written entries
- Poems speaking of blood, murder, Satan, evil, dying or mocking God
- An unusual interest in the Bible without a change in behavior (many people read the Bible to learn about Satan or to blaspheme the Scriptures by mocking them or writing them backwards)
- The "Satanic Bible" or "Satanic Rituals" by Anton LaVey,

books by Aleister Crowley or other books, magazines, comics or writings with heavy occult themes

- Interest in occult-related movies and video games
- Obsession with fantasy role playing games like Dungeons and Dragons, Tunnels and Trolls, etc.
- He/she is called by a different name by friends
- Talking in rhyme
- Boys growing long fingernails
- Previously unnoticed cuts, marks, tattoos, or brands on the body (These are often in obscure places like the buttocks, genitals, breasts etc. and often on the left side of the body)
- Eating raw meat
- Unusually violent rebellion
- Occult paraphernalia like bones, animal skulls, knives, candles (particularly black, red, white), pentagrams, hooded robes, etc.
- Evidence of animal torture or sacrifice

If you discover someone you love is dabbling in Satanism or the occult, let them know you love them and are concerned about their well being. Warn of the dangers associated with Satanism, witchcraft and occult practices. Contact your pastor, your Christian friends, anyone that knows how to pray and get them on it immediately. Take Authority, if it is a child under your Authority, bind those demonic spirits in the name of Jesus. Dabbling in Satanism is not usually just a phase your child will outgrow.

Do not turn to mediums or wizards; do not seek them out, and so make yourselves unclean by them: I am the Lord your God.
Leviticus 19:31

Witchcraft of the Heart

Only a few days after I decided to write this book, I asked the Lord if there was anything else I needed to know about witchcraft and demonic activity. I did the ol' spin it, flip it, fan through it thing I do with my Bible and viola, I opened to 1 Sam 15,

> *For rebellion is like the sin of divination, and arrogance is like the wickedness of idolatry.* 1 Sam 15:23

The Holy Spirit began showing me other types of behavior that are, also, forms of witchcraft and a conduit for demonic spirits. If left unchecked, this behavior would assuredly give up one's Authority and allow demonic spirits free access to them. These all come out of our heart and are things that we have not properly addressed or things that the enemy has sown in us over time.

> *The night is far spent, the day is at hand: let us cast off the works of darkness, and put on the armor of light. Let us walk honestly, as in the day; not in rioting and drunkenness, not in sexual immorality and WANTONNESS, not in strife and envying.* Romans 13: 12 -13

In the word demonic behaviors are sometimes referred to as 'the works of the flesh,' but like all behavior, good and bad, they begin in and come out of the heart. The following is a list of demonic behaviors that are referenced throughout the Bible:

Rebellion / Disobedience
Manipulation / Seduction / Intimidation
Arrogance / Pride / Indignance / Vanity
Sexual Immorality / Adultery / Fornication / Lust
Impurity / Debauchery / Licentiousness / Lewdness
Hatred / Rage / Anger / Resentment / Bitterness
Discord/ Rivalries / Divisions / Factions / Quarreling
Drunkenness / Revelries / Carousing
Self-Seeking / Greed
Envy / Jealousy / Strife
Slander / Gossip / Backbiting
Wantonness / Restlessness / Boredom
Doubt / Unbelief
Fear / Anxiety / Worry

Do a self-evaluation test here and honestly determine if you have even the slightest inclination of any one of them, and if so, repent, confess, bind and cast it to the pit, never to return again. If a believer is behaving like any one of these, that person is not walking in love, but in the flesh. By engaging in this behavior, they are either not loving people or they do not love their Father.

For those who live according to the flesh set their minds on the things of the flesh, but those who live according to the Spirit set their minds on the things of the Spirit. Romans 8:5

Do not love the world or the things in the world. If anyone loves the world, the love of the Father is not in him. 1 Jn. 2:15

This verse is not saying that the Father does not love you, it is saying that by acting in such a manner, you don't love the

Father. The word for love here is, Agape, and it means, to prefer. The verse actually reads like this: ***Do not (Prefer) the world or the things in the world. If anyone (Prefers) the world, they don't (Prefer) the Father.*** By loving the world and all its lustful pleasures, we show our allegiance. By our preference, our loyalty is established.

It is possible there are more demonically inspired behaviors, but this is all I could confirm in the Word, so that is what I am going with. You will notice, everything that we have done in The Altar of Love is rooted and grounded in the Word. Each leg of The Altar of Love is Word-based, with multiple confirmations. Not one iota of The Altar of Love is my opinion. If I have an opinion, I will state as such. Remember, there are two forms of Word; there is the Logos, which is the written Word and there is the Rhema, which is the spoken Word. One is not weightier than the other.

The acts of the flesh are obvious: sexual immorality, impurity, and debauchery; idolatry and sorcery; hatred, discord, jealousy, and rage; rivalries, divisions, factions, and envy; drunkenness, carousing. Gal 5:20

But for those who are self-seeking and who reject the truth and follow wickedness, there will be wrath and anger. Romans 2:8

But if you have bitter jealousy and selfish ambition in your hearts, do not boast in it or deny the truth. Such wisdom does not come from above, but is earthly, unspiritual, demonic. For where jealousy and selfish ambition exist, there will be disorder and every evil practice... James 3:14-16

For God is not a God of confusion but of peace... 1 Cor. 14:33

For I am afraid that when I come, I may not find you as I wish, and you may not find me as you wish. I fear that there may be quarreling, jealousy, rage, rivalry, slander, gossip, arrogance, and disorder. 2 Corinthians 12:20

If any of you lacks wisdom, he should ask God, who gives generously to all without finding fault, and it will be given to him. But he must ask in faith, without doubting, because he who doubts is like a wave of the sea, blown and tossed by the wind. That man should not expect to receive anything from the Lord. He is a double-minded man, unstable in all his ways. James 1:5-8

How to Evict Unwanted Demonic Guests that were Granted Access Through Occult Activity

For You do not delight in sacrifice, or I would bring it; You take no pleasure in burnt offerings. The sacrifices of God are a broken spirit; a broken and a contrite heart, O God, You will not. Psalm 51:17-18

Despite the fact that the law demanded they do sacrifices and offerings for their sin, God is saying that He never delighted in them, in the first place. God cares about the condition of your heart more than anything, and if you are truly sorry for what you have done, He is quick to forgive.

If your unwanted guest has gained access through prior occult practice, you have assuredly given your Authority to the spirit to enter you. It has every legal right to stay and you could rebuke it until your rebuker wears out, but it won't do a thing, because as long as it has Authority, it doesn't have to go anywhere. The way to get Authority back and evict your unwanted guest is twofold. First, one must repent and ask forgiveness for the thing that gave up your Authority in the first place. Second, is to command them to go. Once confession is made, Authority is removed from the beast and handed back to you. You can follow the pattern of prayer below, but it does not have to be verbatim, it just has to imply repentance and forgiveness.

Repentance and Forgiveness: Say, "Father, in the name of Jesus, I repent for (name the activity here), forgive me please, for I did not know what I was doing." (Repentance implies that you will stop the behavior and not do it again, while confession returns Authority back to you.)

If we confess our sins, he is faithful and just to forgive us our sins, and to cleanse us from all unrighteousness. 1 John 1:9

If you engaged in the activity more times than you can remember, do not worry. You can be general and speak to any and all such spirits that entered you through the use of ouija boards, as an example.

Removal of the unwanted beast: This part is a little more involved. Remember, that you have Authority and when you have Authority, you do not ask the Father to do what is in your Authority to do. **You** are doing the commanding. You are not asking it to go, you are demanding it to go. Now that repentance and confession have been made, it does not have the legal right to stay.

Say, "Father, Your Word says, whatever I bind on Earth, is bound in Heaven, therefore, in the name of Jesus, I bind the works, powers, plans, lies and deceptions of the enemy. I bind every power, principality, ruler of darkness, spiritual host of wickedness in Heavenly places, all familiar spirits, all unclean spirits and any such spirits that were granted access to me through (list the occult activity here). I command them to be removed from me now in the name of Jesus, to be bound in chains, torn limb from limb, decapitated, castrated, cast to Hell, where each limb and member will burn at 10,000 degrees in a separate pit, never to be rejoined, never to be released, and never to return again. Father, your Word says that this affliction shall not return a second time."

Why so violent? You have to send a message that they will hear loud and clear. There are billions of those buggers, and Satan will send more your way. You can bet on it. However, this is how it went down in Hell when you took Authority and sent them packing. Satan, seeing the spirit that was assigned to you being cast into his pit says, "What are you doing here? I assigned you to Tommy G. Now, you get back there and do our job or else?" Satan's minion responds, "You don't understand, he knows his Authority. Look at me. I have no head, where are my arms, nooooooooooo." Satan says, "Ok, you two, go get Tommy G before he figures out how to use his Authority."

After casting out all the demons, do not forget to replace them with whatever the person is needing, whatever is missing, especially when considering what was cast out. When the demon is removed it leaves a void for something to replace it and this is where loosing comes in. Whatever is needed, whatever is missing, that is what you loose. Things you can loose are: Wisdom, peace, restraint, discipline, energy, courage, grace, mercy, virtue, love, selflessness, humility, honor, faithfulness, righteousness, joy, tender mercies, loving kindness, integrity, and on and on and on. Whatever that person needs, as long as it lines up with the Word, loose it upon them.

Beloved, do not be surprised at the fiery trial that has come upon you, as though something strange were happening to you. 1 Peter 4:12

Yes, it is likely that you will be tested. Satan is looking to see if you have the testicles for the job. The difference is this: the spirits he will send to test you do not have Authority to enter you unless you immediately turn around and give it back, but I'm assuming that's not going to happen. Hence the importance of repentance, which simply means, stop doing it and don't do it again. This time, all they have is suggestive powers, which are nothing compared to the power and influence they had while inside you. The dynamics have changed, but you're not out of the woods yet. These buggers are very crafty and relentless. Be ready to pray about everything for the next few days... EVERYTHING! Bind everything that appears to be unnatural, even if it's not demonic. Better to be safe than sorry.

Will it ever end? Yes and no. They will eventually leave you alone for awhile if you stand firm. Bind everything that comes your way, and have them ripped to shreds and cast to Hell. You see, these beasts are working multiple schemes. They could have 20 or 30 different plots working at any one time and they are extremely patient, having been working some plots for over a decade. When they were taken off that duty to mess with you, and you had them cast to a pit, never to get out, you just ruined all their other schemes. You just foiled all their other plots, plans they've been working for decades. You really did a number on them, and every time they mess with you and you give them the same treatment, eventually, they will stop, but only for a season. You see, they know us better than we know ourselves. They know we will get lazy and forget all about this stuff, if they leave us alone for awhile. Jesus illustrates this in Mark 4, the Parable of the Sower. I said it earlier and I'll say it again, all spiritual wisdom and knowledge either comes out of the sower or goes back to the sower. In Mark 4:18 – 19 Jesus says, ***Still others are like the seeds sown among the thorns. They hear the word, but the cares of this life, the deceitfulness of wealth, and the desire for other things come in and choke the word, and it becomes unfruitful.***

In the previous verses 16-17, Jesus is describing Satan's attack on new Christians and how most of them fall and go back to the world. In verses 18-19, Jesus is describing a more mature believer that has gotten past the enemy's initial onslaught. But Satan is cunning. He changes his tactics to a more subtle approach designed to choke the Word that is in already our hearts.

That's why I recommend you begin teaching this immediately. Keep it in the forefront of your mind, and never lose it, because it will assuredly save your life one day.

Chapter Ten

Dealing with Sin, Sexual and Other

...But the man who was healed did not know who it was, for Jesus had slipped away while the crowd was there. Afterward, Jesus found the man at the temple and said to him, See, you have been made well. Stop sinning, or something worse may happen to you. John 5:13-14

Here we see Jesus confirming that sin is one of the open doors for sickness and disease. Are we going to mess up and sin occasionally? Absolutely. This is where repentance and confession come in. Remember, God loves a contrite heart more than an arrogant one. God called David a man after His own heart. David committed adultery and murder, and tried to cover it up. How is that a man after the heart of God?

David's sin was not the issue with God. He knows we are mortal, and He, also, knows we are stuck here with a monster. Sure, God would prefer we be as righteous as He is righteous, but it's what we do after we sin that He's most concerned about. Once the prophet Nathan confronted David with his sin, it was David's heartfelt sorrow that God loved. If we are perfect in our behavior, but our attitude is such that we look down on others not so perfect, or we exalt our perfection in front of other to make ourselves look good, we are detestable to the Father.

Let's contrast King David's response to sin with King Uzziah's response in 2 Chronicles chapter 26. It says, *And Uzziah did what was right in the sight of the Lord, and as long as he sought the Lord, God made him prosper.* He had over 2000 mighty men of valor as generals over an army of 300,000. Uzziah provided shields, spears, helmets, coats of armor, bows, and sling stones for the entire army. In Jerusalem, he made devices invented for use on the towers and on the corner defenses, so that soldiers could shoot arrows and hurl large stones from the walls. His fame spread far and wide, for he was greatly helped by the Lord until he became powerful.

But after Uzziah became powerful, his pride led to his downfall. He was unfaithful to the Lord God, and entered the temple of the Lord to burn incense on The Altar. Azariah, the priest with eighty other courageous priests of the Lord followed him in. They confronted King Uzziah and said, "It is not right for you, Uzziah, to burn incense to the Lord. That is for the priests, the descendants of Aaron who have been consecrated to burn incense. Leave the sanctuary, for you have been unfaithful, and you will not be honored by the Lord God."

Uzziah, who had a censer in his hand ready to burn incense, became angry. While he was raging at the priests in their presence before the incense altar in the Lord's temple, leprosy broke out on his forehead. King Uzziah had leprosy, until the day he died.

The sacrifice pleasing to God is a broken spirit. He will not despise a broken and humbled heart. Psalm 51:17

God loves a humble, contrite heart. Humility is the only difference between David and Uzziah. David humbled himself in his sin, but pride rose up in Uzziah and he became angry. Two different responses to sin produced two different outcomes.

The Lord is close to those who are of a broken heart and saves such as are crushed with sorrow for sin and are humbly and thoroughly penitent. Psalm 34:17

Sin is a very difficult issue that most people and churches just do not want to address. I understand, it's very condemning. It forces us to look inward when it's so much easier to look outward. I was reading Psalms with a friend of mine, just recently, when I noticed David ranting about someone that was causing him trouble. He kept telling God to smite his enemy, destroy their posterity, and make an utter end to their existence, as well as, their heritage. Then, in the next breath, he says, but as for me, have mercy on me, be gentle with me, don't judge me too harshly. Isn't that just how we are, too? We demand people be held accountable for even the smallest offense, but we expect mercy when we totally mess up.

One main problem with sin is the fact that people who commit it (everybody), want to just push it in the past and forget about it. The Lord showed me clearly that this way of thinking is dangerous. Sin needs to be repented for and confessed. I know I mentioned it earlier, but it is so important, I must mention it again. Not all sin is the same.

> *Flee from sexual immorality. Every other sin a man can commit is outside his body, but he who sins sexually sins against his own body.* 1 Corinth 6:18

Every sin other than sexual sin is outside the body, but sexual sin is a direct assault on your physical person, and nobody controls it but you. In the time I have spent taking people through The Altar of Love, almost all their physical ailments were rooted either in the occult or in sexual sin. Sexual sin left unaddressed causes sickness and disease, many years later.

It's all about the Relationship

Sin left unconfessed or unrepented for, gives up our Authority and opens the door for the enemy to enter. One of his most effective schemes is to induce guilt, and guilt left unchecked will create separation. Separation from the Father is what Satan needs to take you down. Separation breaks fellowship moving us away from the protection of the Father. Think of it like this... you are walking next to Jesus as He holds an umbrella that is big enough for the two of you. The sin brings guilt, the guilt brings separation, and now you are walking out from under the umbrella protection of the Father. He's telling you to come back where it is safe and dry, but the guilt won't let you.

As in David's case, and as God Himself said in Psalm 34, **God loves a humble, penitent heart.** The best and safest place for us when we sin is at The Altar. Satan will heap loads of discouragement, like, "You're not worthy, you always do that, you'll never break free, you're a loser, you're a hypocrite, you might as well just give up already. This Christianity stuff doesn't work, it's definitely not for you, look how many times you commit the same offense, this is just how you were made, just go with the flow already." He can make a Spirit Filled Believer feel so inferior within a few days, that they will actually begin to contemplate the deceptive suggestions.

The most important thing to do when you realize you messed up and sinned, is go directly to the throne, repent, and ask forgiveness. Take back your Authority, bind the enemy and cast him to the pit. Next, spend some time in prayer and praise.

Never, I repeat, never let anything come between you and your relationship with the Father.

One of the biggest problems with the Once Saved, Always Saved doctrine is that they feel like they do not need to repent or confess for their sin. Their false belief that they can do anything and it will have no bearing on their eternal salvation, makes them arrogant. Arrogance leads to pride, and pride leads to the fall. Foolishly, they have been deceived into thinking they can sin willy-nilly, and there are no repercussions. Nothing could be farther from the truth. Sin, no matter how small, must be repented for and confessed. David went so far as to ask the Father to cleanse him of secret faults. Secret faults are sins that he was committing, but he didn't even know he was doing it. Now, that's dedication.

I repeat, all sin must be confessed and repented for and repentance should be a daily process. As I take people through The Altar of Love, I have them make a list of the sin they can remember. As well, I encourage that you get in a quiet place and spend some time asking the Father to reveal anything you may have forgotten from your past that He wants you to confess. And when I say confess, I am saying that we need to apologize for our sin. Not just saying sorry, but asking God to forgive us just as Jesus asked the Father to forgive those who were crucifying Him. You will find that things start coming back to your memory at different times. When they do, just be quick to confess it, repent, and ask forgiveness.

Not everyone who says to me, Lord, Lord, will enter the kingdom of Heaven, but the one who does the will of my Father who is in Heaven. On that day, many will say to me, Lord, Lord, did we not prophesy in your name, and cast out demons in your name, and do many mighty works in your name? And then will I declare to them, I never knew you; depart from me, you workers of lawlessness. Matthew 7:23

Knew - Strong's #1097 ginōskō = sexual intimacy. Also, used in Luke 1:34, *And Mary said to the angel, How can this be since I do not know a man?*

Our Father desires a relationship with us more than anything, but our guilt causes us to hide from Him like Adam and Eve hid in the garden. Guilt drives us away from the only source that can protect us while we are in the dangerous aftermath of sin. The best place for us at a time like that is at The Altar of God, but Satan knows the sin gives him a small window of opportunity to bring guilt and shame, which brings separation, and that is where the real danger is. Just how far into despair Satan can bring us is dependent upon what sin we committed and how guilty he can make us feel about it.

The absolute best example of this is as if you loaned a good friend $1,500. They promised to pay you back and normally they are very responsible, but unforeseen circumstances may have caused a delay in that repayment. With the delay, a distance begins to emerge until not only are they no longer in contact with you, but they are, also, avoiding your attempt to reach them. Now this isn't just any friend, this is your best friend for years and years and you really do not care about the money. The friendship is way more valuable than $1,500, but the guilt makes them ashamed and they are unable to face you until it's paid.

That is exactly how Satan uses sin to separate us from God. First, he brings guilt, then he makes us feel ashamed.

Eventually, a distance grows between you and your Father. We're dealing with the master of guilt and shame here, and he is not content to stop there. He'll use the guilt to get them to feel hopeless, which will lead them into even worse sin. The best thing you can do for your friend here is just forgive the debt altogether. Likewise, God has given us repentance and confession, so all our sins will be forgiven. Forgiveness wipes away guilt and shame.

The OSAS message is much more dangerous than meets the eye. The false grace gospel, also, implies a false sense of relationship, because relationships are forged when the two relating parties fellowship. The OSAS doctrine assumes there is no need for repentance or forgiveness, or anything for that matter. Many, not all, but many OSAS believers have a very superficial relationship with their Father, mainly, because they feel no need to fellowship with Him.

Children who recognize the commandments and understand the purpose of repentance are constantly going to the Father two, three, four, or more times a day. All this creates a bond between the two parties that begins to grow into a more loving relationship. Eventually, the offending party begins to mature in their walk with Christ. The deep love they have from all the time spent together, has now made it so that they no longer want to walk in willful sin, because they don't want to disappoint their Father. Repentance draws you to your Father and shows Him your loving heart, while His forgiveness towards you shows His love to you. A love affair develops, because God loves a humble and contrite heart.

If we look more closely at Matthew 7:23, *Not everyone who says to me, 'Lord, Lord,' will enter the kingdom of Heaven,* we see something nobody is talking about. Whenever we read our Bible, we must carefully consider who is being written to, so we can properly understand the meaning. Is He talking to a Jew, a believer or an unbeliever? Well, who calls Jesus Lord? Do Jews, do Muslims, do Buddhists, do evolutionists or atheists or even agnostics? No, no, no and no. The only people that call Jesus Lord are people that 'think' they are Christians. Therefore, Jesus is really saying, "Not everyone who calls themselves a Christian will enter the Kingdom of Heaven." Are you beginning to see it yet?

If we understand that 'to know' our Lord Jesus is to have a close, intimate relationship with Him, but what does that even look like? Saying a 'sinner's prayer,' is not 'knowing' God. Being raised in a Christian home and being forced to go to church is not 'knowing' God. Volunteering at church or homeless shelters is not 'knowing' God. Giving tithes and offerings is not 'knowing' God. Christian bumper stickers, Christian clothing, Christian jewelry, and listening to Christian music, is not 'knowing' God. Knowing God and knowing Jesus is treating them like you would a best friend, the friend you call and tell everything that's going on in your life, the one you talk to when you first get up, the last one you talk to when you go to sleep, the one you tell all your secrets to, and the one you confide in when you mess up.

He who loves father or mother more than Me is not worthy of Me; and he who loves son or daughter more than Me is not worthy of Me. Matthew 10:37

To 'know' your Father is proven by the time you spend with Him. Example: If a man takes his wife to a sporting event with his friends, but spends all his time socializing with his friends, not his wife, she's not going to consider that intimate time spent with her. Taking her to dinner and lavishing all his attention on her and only her, making her feel like she is the most important person in the world to him, is intimate time together. That's what our Father wants. He wants our time, and not just the drowsy, last minute and a half you grudgingly give Him when you lay your head down at night. This is a love relationship and it needs to be treated as such. God is not your grandpa, and He's not happy with us jumping in His lap, and digging through His pockets for some spare change, so we can run to the store and get a snack. I implore you to develop a close intimate relationship with your Father, with your Jesus, because your eternal life depends upon it.

Make time for Him by setting your alarm fifteen minutes earlier, so you can read your Bible before your day starts. Talk to Him like you talk to a friend. Tell him how you feel, what you think, and ask Him for His advice about stuff. He loves that and He will respond back to you, which is the best part of it. The more you do it, the more you will want to. Your Father and your King Jesus don't just love you, but They're "in love" with you. There's a huge difference. I try to love people, but it's not the same as being "in love" with someone you can lavish your time, your effort, and your energy upon. Jesus is "in love" with us and He wants us to be "in love" with Him, too.

Think about it. How would you feel if you were madly in love with your spouse, but they didn't love you back? The honeymoon has worn off and now they treat you like a roommate. Oh, they say they love you, but you know they don't, because of the way they act towards you. They never make time for you and when they do, their attention is on something or someone else. That's a horrible feeling, and it's a feeling Jesus feels every day about most of his bride. That is exactly why He is saying, **Go away, I never knew you**. I urge you, with every part of my being. Fall back in love with Jesus, because you don't ever want to hear those words.

> *Jesus said, If you want to enter eternal life, keep the commandments.* Matt 19:17

> *His precepts (commandments) are trustworthy.*
>
> *They are upheld forever.* Psalm 111:8

If God says something lasts forever, He's not going to abolish it. Jesus confirms this on multiple occasions, when He tells us to keep the commandments and do the Will of the Father.

> *Not everyone who says to me, 'Lord, Lord,' will enter the kingdom of Heaven, but the one who does the will of my Father, who is in Heaven.* Matthew 7:23

As is the case with occult activity, your past and/or present sin either has or will open the door for many demonic spirits to have legal access. Just in case you do not know how to judge this for yourself, use the ten commandments first.

I. You shall have no other God's before Me.

II. You shall not make idols.

III. You shall not take the name of the LORD your God in vain.

IV. Remember the Sabbath day, to keep it holy.

V. Honor your father and your mother.

VI. You shall not murder.

VII. You shall not commit adultery.

VIII. You shall not steal.

IX. You shall not bear false witness against your neighbor.

X. You shall not covet

Once you get an understanding of the Ten Commandments, and familiarize yourself with following them, transition over into the two that Jesus said to use: Love God and love your neighbor, because Love covers all ten. However, there is an added level of expected righteousness within the commandment of love. You see, before the cross, they only sinned if they broke one of the ten commandments, by physically engaging in the activity. It is much more difficult now, because Jesus said, even if we lust in our heart, we commit adultery. Therefore, we are now judged by our thoughts, as well as, our actions.

Let me reiterate... Don't get frustrated thinking you might as well give up, because you cannot do that. No, that is why God gave us the gifts of repentance and forgiveness, to use them daily. I am not saying you have to pray for salvation daily, I'm saying you need to repent and ask forgiveness daily. Look at it like this, if we are repenting and asking for forgiveness daily, what are we doing? We're in prayer, right where He wants us. So, the sin that Satan was going to try to use to divide you from your Father is the very thing God will use to draw you closer to Him. What am I saying? Sin is good, because it draws us closer to God? God forbid, no, but that it may be used to accomplish in us what was missing all along, intimacy. This is the thing He wants from us more than anything, a relationship.

Repentance and forgiveness: Say, "Father, in the name of Jesus, I repent for (name the sin here), forgive me please, for I did not know what I was doing."

If you engaged in the activity on multiple occasions, be general and speak to any and all such spirits that entered you through the sinful activity in general, not necessarily each and every incident.

Removal of the unwanted beast: Once repentance and confession is made, you have re-established your Authority over the unwanted beast. **Do not** ask the Father to make them go for you, because it is your responsibility to do it. **You** are doing the commanding. **You are not asking** it to go, **you are demanding it to go**. Now that repentance and confession have been made, it does not have the legal right to stay. You are the law now.

Say, "Father, Your Word says, whatever I bind on Earth, is bound in Heaven, therefore, in the name of Jesus, I bind the works, powers, plans, lies and deceptions of the enemy. I bind every power, principality, ruler of darkness, spiritual host of wickedness in heavenly places, all familiar spirits, all unclean spirits, and any such spirits that were granted access to me through (list the sin here), I command them to come out of me now in the name of Jesus, to be bound in chains, torn limb from limb, decapitated, castrated, cast to hell where each limb and member will burn at 10,000 degrees in separate pits, never to be rejoined, never to be released and never to return again. Father, your Word says that this affliction shall not return a second time."

Now, commence loosing what is missing in the personality that maybe didn't cause it, but sure made it easier for the demon to manifest itself more powerfully. Anytime you evict a varmint, there is a void to fill. This is where loosing comes into play. Jesus said, **_Whatever you loose on earth is loosed in Heaven._** Let me give an example:

I came across a young girl working the counter at a burger joint one day. As I approached her, I heard the Holy Spirit tell me she needed prayer, so before she said a word, I said, "You need prayer for something. What is it?" She responded, "I've been diagnosed just recently with schizophrenia." Immediately, I raised my hand to put it on her head and as I did, she leaned into me giving me Authority to do it. I said, "In the name of Jesus, I bind schizophrenia. You cannot have this girl. Come out now, in Jesus' name, **and I loose upon her the Mind of Christ.** I declare and decree from this day forth, she is free from schizophrenia, for whom the Son sets free, is free indeed."

Normally, I would have been more thorough and made sure I addressed other issues or spirits as not to leave anything behind, but I could see her manager behind her watching me very intently, so I needed to wrap it up before Satan could muck it up with a scene. I looked for her to see how she was doing when my burger was done, but she was working the drive-thru window now, so I just sat down and ate.

When I finished, I went to put my tray away at the counter and noticed her looking at me from the drive-thru window. She took off the headset and came running at me and body slammed me with a huge hug. With her head buried in my chest she said, "Thank you, thank you, thank you. You have no idea. Thank you." She leaned back and told me how she has not been able to think normally for about a year. She couldn't keep a job and was failing school, but for the first time, in a long time she can think clearly again. She was crying and telling me how she called her praying Christian grandmother and told her about this guy that laid his hand on her head and prayed over her and set her free. She told her grandmother that she would be going to church with her from now on.

You may have noticed, after casting out the spirit of schizophrenia, I loosed the mind of Christ. Schizophrenia removed leaves a perfect void for something to replace it. This is where loosing comes in. Whatever is needed, whatever is missing, that is what you loose. Other things you can loose are: wisdom, peace, restraint, discipline, energy, courage, grace, mercy, virtue, love, selflessness, humility, honor, faithfulness, righteousness, joy, tender mercies, loving kindness, integrity, and on and on. Whatever that person needs, as long as it lines up with the Word, loose it upon them. A more extensive list will be provided in a later chapter.

Sexual Sin

Sexual sin is on a whole different level than other sin, not because I say so, but because the Word tells us so. I put it in a category all its own, but it's similar to that of occult practices, because it involves blood, and anything that involves blood is a sacrifice to Satan. Semen is the origin of the blood for the baby. When the Holy Spirit impregnated Mary, Jesus was born with the blood of His Father. Whether you realize it or not, you are making a blood covenant with Satan when having sex outside marriage, and that is primarily what God says in 1 Corinthians.

I wrote you not to associate with anyone who claims to be a brother or sister and is sexually immoral or greedy, an idolater or verbally abusive, a drunkard or a swindler. Do not even eat with such a person. 1 Cor. 5:11

Understand that Paul is talking to believers about believers. He is not talking about avoiding worldly people. Otherwise, we'd have to leave the planet. No, he is talking about people that call themselves Christians. If we are fellowshipping with believers that are actively engaging in fornication, adultery, drunkenness, revelries and the like, it will desensitize us and we'll start behaving like them. When he says we are not to eat with them, he is saying we are not to be intimately acquainted with them. They are not the kind of people we should be spending our time with. He goes on to say:

Or do you not know that the unrighteous will not inherit the Kingdom of God? Do not be deceived; neither fornicators, nor idolaters, nor adulterers, nor effeminate, nor homosexuals, nor thieves, nor the greedy, nor drunkards, nor revilers, nor swindlers will inherit the Kingdom of God. 1 Corinthians 6:9

This is not difficult to understand. Again I remind you, **Paul is talking to believers** about people that falsely assumed they were believers and he's calling them unrighteous, saying they will not enter the Kingdom of God. Paul understood the spiritual consequences of sexual sin, so well that he reiterated it just in case they didn't understand the seriousness of the covenant they were making with the enemy. He said:

Flee from sexual immorality. Every other sin a man commits is outside his body, but he who sins sexually sins against his own body. 1 Cor. 6:20

That word "flee" means to escape with your life. In the strong's concordance it states: 'To be saved by flight, to escape to safety out of absolute danger. ABSOLUTE DANGER!' Sexual sin is considered absolute danger? Why absolute danger? Because your salvation literally hangs in the balance here. Then it says:

> *Or do you not know that he who is joined to a prostitute becomes one body with her? As it is written, The two will become one flesh.* 1 Cor. 6:16

Can it get any more clear? Sex outside marriage is like joining the Holy Spirit to a whore, and He's just not going to allow that. Paul's reference to a whore is more significant that it's surface meaning. He is comparing sex outside marriage to having sex with one of the Satanic whores in the temple where they worshipped all their demonic God's. In Paul's day, it was a form of worship and sacrifice to Satan and not only are we exposing ourselves to horrible diseases down the road, but your Father views it as you committing adultery on Him and the consequences are grave to say the least.

> *Do not banish me from your presence, and don't take your Holy Spirit from me.* Psalm 51:11

It is possible for God to banish us from His presence and take His spirit from us and sexual sin, as well as, occult activity will do just that. God will not allow His Holy Spirit to be joined to a whore.

> *Do you not know that your body is a temple of the Holy Spirit who is in you, whom you have received from God? You are not your own; you were bought for a price. Therefore glorify God with your body.* 1 Cor. 6:19-20

We either glorify God in our bodies through restraint from sexual sin, or we glorify Satan with a blood sacrifice by sexual immorality. It's our choice.

I call Heaven and earth as witnesses against you today that I have set before you life and death, blessing and cursing. So choose life, so that you and your descendants may live.
Deut 30:19

How sweet is God? First, He gives us free will to make our own choices, but just in case we don't know what the right choice is, He tells us what we should choose, because He loves us and wants the best for us. How many of us have done the exact same thing with our own kids? They come to us with a dilemma and we give them our opinion, one we have formed over of years of experience, so we know exactly how it will play out. But all we can do is offer our advice, because they have the ultimate choice.

Divorce

To the married I give this command (not I, but the Lord): A wife must not separate from her husband. But if she does, she must remain unmarried or else be reconciled to her husband. And a husband must not divorce his wife. 1 Corinthians 7:10

When Paul says, "Not I, but the Lord," he is saying that this is not his opinion, but that command comes directly from Jesus.

And some Pharisees came up to him, testing him, and began to question him, whether it was lawful for a man to divorce a wife, saying, "Is it lawful for a man to divorce his wife **for any cause at all**?" And He answered and said to them, "**What did Moses command you?**" And they said, "Moses permitted a man to

215

write a certificate of divorce and send her away." (Note: Remember Jesus' reply, *What did Moses command?* This event is before the cross, and this law will change after the cross, because Jesus abolished the Law of Moses on the cross.)

And He answered and said, *Have you not read, that He who created them [but] from the beginning of creation made them male and female, and said, 'for this cause a man shall leave his father and mother, and shall cleave to his wife, and the two shall become one flesh?* Consequently, **they are no longer two, but one flesh. "<u>What God has joined together, let no man separate</u>."**

They said to him, "Why, then, did Moses' command to give her a certificate and send her away?" Jesus said to them, *Because of your hardness of heart, he wrote you this commandment, so Moses permitted you to divorce your wives; but from the beginning it has not been this way. And I say to you, whoever divorces his wife, except for immorality, and marries another woman commits adultery.*

The Jewish men were notorious for using their wives up in their youth and discarding them for a newer version and they begged Moses to make it lawful to ease their conscience. Moses was just appeasing the sinful lust of their hardened hearts. The real issue here is what nobody is acknowledging, the Word says, *Christ has redeemed us from the curse of the law.* If we are no longer under the law of Moses, then we are under God's Law and the only provision for divorce in God's Law is Adultery. Anything else will cause both parties to be committing adultery on God, if they divorce and remarry, which is why He tells us to remain unmarried if we divorce).

And in the house, the disciples began to question Him about this again and He said to them, *Whoever divorces his wife, and marries another woman commits adultery against her, and if she herself divorces her husband and marries another man, she is committing adultery.* The person that is doing the divorcing, if it is being done for any other reason except sexual immorality, is committing adultery. And as we learned in the section regarding sexual sin, adultery is a blood sacrifice to Satan. If you were involved in a divorce that wasn't the result of adultery, repent and ask forgiveness; plead the blood of Jesus and cancel the covenant with Satan.

If we deliberately go on sinning after we have received the knowledge of the truth, no further sacrifice for sins remains, but only a fearful expectation of judgment and raging fire... Heb 10:26

Clearly, Paul is talking to believers and including himself in the conversation when he says, "we," and "a fearful expectation of judgment and raging fire," sounds a lot like Hell. Before we get saved, we are not sinning deliberately, we are sinning ignorantly. We don't know squat, but after we are saved and we come to the knowledge of the truth, mature Christians really don't have an excuse any longer. We can't claim ignorance, or even stupidity for that matter. Jesus said, *If you love me, keep my commandments.*

Chapter Eleven

Dealing with Witches, Curses and Spells etc.

...the LORD turned the curse into a blessing for you, because the LORD your God loves you. Deut 23:5

One very important list in The Altar of Love involves associations with occult persons and/or places, past and present. I cannot stress this enough, you are the sheriff, with the badge, the gun, and the backup SWAT team (angels). You are the judge, jury and executioner. FEAR NOT! Unless you hand them your Authority, they have no power over you, whatsoever, only parlor tricks. You have the ultimate Superpower... you have AUTHORITY!

The Spirit of God, who raised Jesus from the dead, lives in you. Rom. 8:11

When Jesus was in the presence of demons, they shuddered in fear, and if the same Spirit of Jesus lives in you, it only stands to reason that they are just as afraid of you. But this is only true if you know your Identity as a Child of God and walk in Authority. This section is all about confidence. I cannot stress this enough, all they have is parlor tricks. There is nothing they can do to harm you, but you have to be confident in who you are as a Child of the King. This is just another reason a believer must fully understand their Identity.

Look at it like this, you're eight years old and you're being harassed by a 12 year old bully, but this time your 18 year old brother is there behind you. Are you afraid of the bully anymore? Not just no, but hell no. You are as bold as a lion, because you have nothing to fear. You've got backup, and it's waaaaay bigger and badder than the bully.

That's what Jesus meant when He said, **Whatever you bind on Earth, I'll bind in Heaven.** We do the binding and He backs us up with a legion of angels, if necessary, and all the while, He's living inside us. If that doesn't build your confidence, nothing will. Fear not. Only believe, for God has prepared us for this very purpose and has given us His Spirit as a guarantee, because we believed in what we heard and are faithful to do it.

If you suspect that someone has placed a curse, a hex, or a spell on you, in the past or present, do not fret. It has no Authority to stay unless you were a willing participant to the event. Let's address several different scenarios. In the event you were not a co-conspirator to a curse leveled against you, the process is quite simple.

> *Like a fluttering sparrow or a darting swallow, an undeserved curse will not land on its intended victim.*
> Proverbs 26:2

The meaning behind this verse is the answer to the curse itself. Just as the sower sows the word, this verse in Proverbs 26:2, is your Word to sow. Just as sparrows and swallows return to their nests, likewise, a curse that is undeserved must return to the sender unless you have given up your Authority and granted it permission to stay. If you know a person has cast a curse on you and you do nothing and are afraid, fear gives it Authority. The Hebrew word for undeserved in this verse has significant importance, as well. It literally means that you did nothing to deserve it. It, also, implies that you did not give it your Authority to stay.

If the curse was in the form of sickness and you claimed it with your words, you have Authorized it to stay, so you need to:

1) Repent for giving your Authority away,

2) Ask God to forgive you for believing the lie of the enemy,

3) Return the curse to sender, bind and cast away anything that was given Authority

4) Command all symptoms of the disease to go in the name of Jesus, just as we did in the section on sin.

The process remains the same as with occult and sexual sin, except in this case, quote Proverbs 26:2. The curse will then go back to the person who sent it. The reason why is because of what we learned earlier... words, while invisible, are still things that create things, and the things they create are eternal. Who determines if it is deserved or not? The ultimate judge is God and don't forget, you are His child and you hold a special place in His heart. He never rules unfairly, nor does he play favorites. He is always fair and honest.

If you have absolutely no idea that a curse has been placed on you and you have done nothing to deserve it, you have nothing to fear, because it has no power or Authority to stay. **An undeserved curse will not land on its intended victim.** If you suspect an acquaintance, a family member, a co-worker is practicing witchcraft and has a beef with you, be proactive and cover yourself and your loved ones in prayer. Let me give you an example. Pray this:

"Father, Your word says, Like a fluttering sparrow or a darting swallow, an undeserved curse will not land on its intended victim. Therefore, in the name of the Lord Jesus I command any and all curses, hexes, spells etc. to return to sender immediately."

Follow that with:

No weapon formed against me shall prosper; and every tongue that rises against me in judgment I shall condemn.
Isaiah 54:17

Notice that God is instructing us to condemn every tongue that rises against us. This, also, proves that we are in Authority and that God is not going to do it for us. It's our job, so if we don't do it, Satan will, and it gives him the legal right to inflict harm.

This is exactly what Jesus was talking about when He said, *My people perish for lack of knowledge.* Our ignorance of Identity and Authority keeps us in a constant state of bondage and affliction, always needing a miracle just to get back to even. This is the main reason why bad things happen to good Christian people. They have no understanding of their Identity and/or their Authority.

A word study of the Hebrew word for condemn taken from Isaiah 54:17, *I shall condemn,* is quite revealing as well.

Condemn - Strong's #7561 rasha: (raw-shah') inflicted punishment, treat wickedly. Once again, this only serves to confirm that not only are we the sheriff, but we are the judge, jury and executioner. Furthermore, it is instructing us to treat them wickedly when handing out punishment. It is the only thing they know or respect. That is why I tear the demons apart, like a good soldier, I'm only following orders.

Now, finish your prayer with Authority:

"I thank you Father that no weapon formed against me shall prosper and Your Word says that I have the Authority to condemn every tongue that rises against me. Therefore, in the name of Jesus, I declare and decree every plot, plan, trap, snare and lie of the enemy that comes against me (place yourself and/or list other people covered under this prayer) be thwarted and come to nothing. I give no place, no power and no Authority to the enemy. I assume Authority today and I bind every power, principality, ruler of darkness, spiritual host of wickedness in Heavenly places, all familiar spirits, and all unclean spirits that would attempt to assert dominion and Authority over the thoughts and intents of our hearts and our minds. I command all such spirits to come out in the name of Jesus, be bound in chains, torn limb from limb, decapitated, castrated, cast to Hell, where each limb and member will burn at 10,000 degrees in separate pits, never to be rejoined, never to be released and never to return again, in Jesus name. Father, your word says that this affliction shall not return a second time."

At this point, it's time to loose what you desire in place of the entities that were just cast out. For Example:

- where there is sickness, loose health and healing
- where there is despair, loose hope
- where there is lack, loose abundance
- where there is confusion, depression and afflictions of the mind, loose the mind of Christ
- where there is fear, loose power, love, a sound mind and courage

- where there is faithlessness, loose faith
- where there is anger, loose self control and peace
- where there is division or separation, loose restoration
- where there is rebellion and disobedience, loose obedience
- where there is arrogance, pride and indignance, loose humility and love where there is lying, cheating or steeling, loose integrity and honor
- where there is selfishness, loose selflessness and love
- where there is prejudice, loose love and respect
- where there is lust, sexual immorality, adultery and fornication, loose self- control, discipline, virtue, chastity, righteousness and Godliness
- where there is greed and stinginess, loose generosity
- where there is laziness, loose Godly ambition
- where there is weakness, loose strength
- where there is addiction, loose discipline and self-control
- where there is weariness, loose perseverance
- where there is manipulation, seduction or intimidation, loose virtue, submission to the Authority of Jesus and the Word of God
- where there is drunkenness, revelries and carousing, loose peace, love, joy, sobriety, discipline and righteousness
- where there is fatigue, loose energy
- where there is discord, divisions and quarreling, loose reconciliation, restoration, love and peace
- where there is envy and jealousy, loose contentment, peace, love and joy
- where there is slander, backbiting and gossip, loose restraint, discipline, honor, trustworthiness

- where there is boredom, restlessness and wantonness, loose peace, contentment, discipline and honor.

If it is something that you participated in due to youthful foolishness, repent, ask forgiveness for going after strange God's and believing the lie. Take Authority and command them to come out in the name of Jesus. Bind them in chains, tear them apart, cast them to separate pits never to be reunited and never to return.

DANGER! Blood Letting, Blood Covenants, Blood Sacrifices and Tattoos

This is not going to be a very popular section, because so many people have fallen prey to the enemy through tattoos. I have done many cases where the people have actually made a blood covenant with Satan to try to get a specific thing. This is really bad y'all, but the thing is, it's no different than getting a tattoo. Tattoos are a bloodletting sacrifice and the tattoo artist is a Satanic high priest performing the ceremony in a Satanic temple. The good news is, Christ has redeemed us and God is a forgiving God, but He was very specific in his Word about tattoos, because He understands how blood sacrifices such as tattoos give away Authority, so something may gain entrance.

Do not cut your bodies for the dead or put tattoo marks on yourself Lev. 19:28

Cleansing oneself from these spirits has an added step or two, because blood was involved. First, confess the behavior or act. Second, repent and ask forgiveness. Third, plead the blood of Jesus over the covenant that was made with Satan and cancel it, rendering it null and void, in Jesus' name. Fourth, plead the blood of Jesus over a renewed covenant with the Father, Son and Holy Spirit. Fifth, enter in praise, worship and thanksgiving. Sixth, cast them out and rip them to shreds like I stated earlier, always being careful to set the parameters of their punishment to never be allowed back. Seventh, shift the focus on any ailments, sicknesses, symptoms or personality disorders. Command them to come out, send them to Hell, and loose whatever is needed in their place.

Let me warn you, all these demons lay dormant for a time, but they will eventually rear their ugly heads one day. Maybe it'll manifest itself in diabetes that causes one to have their feet amputated, or a debilitating back injury that forces another to quit their job and live on disability. Alzheimer's to claim a beautiful mind, cancer, endometriosis, cystic fibrosis, etc. Repent, assume Authority and live your life in peace, for the Kingdom of Heaven is at hand.

Abortion

Let me begin by saying, your Father loves you and his greatest concern for you is that you are restored back to Him and your baby at all cost. If you had an abortion, your baby is in Heaven and you will care for them when you arrive. Do whatever it takes to get there. Name your baby if you have not done so, otherwise, they're all just called precious. Abortion is, also, a blood covenant with Satan, and a doctor once said, "Every abortionist I know is a Satanist." Abortion was one of the first sins brought to Earth by the 200 angels that originally fell in the Book of Enoch. Like tattoos, Satan requires abortion as a sacrifice to him, because he always copies and perverts what the Father does.

The cleansing steps are the same as tattoos: Repent and ask forgiveness, plead the blood of Jesus over the covenant and cancel it. Plead the blood over a renewed covenant with the Father, Son, and Holy Spirit. Cast out the demons that attached to you through the event and have them torn limb from limb as you cast them to the pit of Hell. Side note, list some of the feelings you may have experienced since the abortion like, guilt, shame, depression, anxiety, anger, resentment, bitterness, suicide, etc. These are demonic spirits that gained entry with Authority, so once you take their Authority away, call them out by name as you tear them apart and cast them to Hell.

Generational Curses

Generational curses are curses that have been passed down from generation to generation. If the disease your child has is the same one your mother has and is the same one her father had, it's definitely a generational curse. It's an Authority issue, and somebody needs to stand in Authority and break the curse.

If a great grandparent dabbled in the occult or committed sexual sin and allowed a spirit to enter them, that spirit, having found a suitable home, will ride that horse, as long as possible, or until they find a newer more suitable host body. What better home is there than families that have no clue what they are dealing with? All a spirit needs to transfer from one person to another is to touch them. Many times, children are the most susceptible, because they have no knowledge of such things and no way to know what is happening to them. Most people in the world have no clue, either, but sometimes the spirit has a difficult time overpowering the personality of the host body to get them to do something against their personal moral code of conduct.

These spirits have to maneuver within the confines of the individual personality, so he's trying to figure out just how far this person will go. Most of the time, it's a slow desensitization of the host body that leads to their destruction. That is why children make great vessels, they are so pliable from their youth. This is just another reason why Satan is undermining the role and Authority of the parents in the home and moving parental rights, more and more away from the parent and to the state. Discipline can force a child to become more obedient to the parent than to the demonic spirit trying to lead them astray. A child left undisciplined will more often than not become a monster to deal with.

Foolishness is bound up in the heart of a child; The rod of discipline will remove it far from him. Proverbs 22:15

Do not hold back discipline from the child, Although you strike him with the rod, he will not die. You shall strike him with the rod And rescue his soul from Sheol. Proverbs 23:13-14

Discipline your son while there is hope, And do not desire his death. Proverbs 19:18

God knew what was up. He knew what was happening in the Spirit realm. He knows how these things work and he left instructions of how to address rebellious children. Some children will side with the demon completely and rebel from any and all parental discipline. Personality traits such as obedience or rebellion, like eye color, are influenced by genetics, as well as, environment and can be passed from parent to child. The genetic makeup of a child is a stronger influence on personality than child rearing, according to a study on more than 350 pairs of identical twins reared in different families after six days of extensive testing that included analysis of blood, brain waves, intelligence and behavioral traits. The findings are the first major results to emerge from a long-term project at the University of Minnesota.

This is why Israel was instructed by God to stone rebellious children. Furthermore, they were instructed to take the children out of the city and do it, so that the spirit could not transfer to another. In doing so, Israel would eventually eliminate the rebellion within the gene pool, or at the least, drastically reduce it. I can attest to this in my own business. I have instructed hundreds of thousands of children from all cultures and the absolute best behaved kids are my Jewish kids, hands down, not even close.

When an unclean spirit goes out of a man, he goes through dry places, seeking rest, and finds none. Then he says, I will return to my house from which I came. And when he comes, he finds his home empty, swept, and put in order. Then he goes and takes with him seven other spirits more wicked than himself, and they enter his home and dwell there; and the last state of that man is worse than the first. So shall it also be with this wicked generation. Matt. 12:43-45

Can you believe that thing actually thinks you are his home? Your attitude should be one of indigence. How dare that thing! Tell it that it is no longer welcome in your home (your body). Say this, "This home, is not your home any more. You've got to go in the name of Jesus." This should infuriate you. It did me when I found out. When you speak to them, do not be polite, this is war. You speak forcefully and demand them to do what you will, because in this phase of the process you are no longer the sheriff, you're the judge, jury, and executioner.

If a person is not saved, if they have not made Jesus the Lord of their life, if they have not spoken with their mouth that He is the Son of God, who died for their sins, who rose again and is seated at the right hand of the Father and believed it in their heart, then I never cast a demon out without leading them to salvation afterwards. It should be an easy task considering they were just under demonic possession. You certainly won't have a difficult time convincing them at least.

Matthew 12:43-45, notice that the home was swept clean, this implies that the Holy Spirit was not there, so the spirit was able to waltz right back into his old home. If it's vacant, if the Holy Spirit does not reside there, it doesn't need anything special to enter, however, if the Holy Spirit is residing there, it needs permission by way of Authority or touch. If it's touch, it has to be in someone first, before it can come to you, and that's highly unlikely. It happens, but it's rare. If it were to happen, you will know almost immediately.

Demonic entities are diametrically opposed to the Holy Spirit that is inside of you and their characteristics will be obvious to notice. You will begin to detect behavioral changes to the extreme, like: anger, anxiety, depression, moodiness, laziness, apathy, insensitivity, selfishness, pain, sickness, doubt, worry, etc.

This is why you have to know yourself well and as it says in 1 Peter 5:8, **Be sober and vigilant...** If you know yourself, you will sense a change in your mood, your behavior, your personality.

No big deal, just slide away somewhere and take Authority over it, cast it out, rip it to shreds, send it to Hell, never to return again. If it does not leave immediately, assume you gave up your Authority somehow, figure out what it was, repent, ask forgiveness and then start casting it out. You're the judge, get creative. It's the only thing they respect.

If spirits can transfer by touch, should we be worried about touching people? No, if that spirit has found a pliable host, they are likely to stay put unless they are on a specific assignment against you, but that's not likely unless you are doing something to destroy Satan's kingdom. Something like The Altar of Love, ha ha! If you took this lesson and began to do it for people, eventually, you'd be targeted, but as long as you are sober and vigilant, you'll be fine. As well, once you begin ripping them to shreds, they are in no hurry to mess with you. They certainly don't want to end up like their co-workers, dismembered and burning at 10,000 degrees.

Chapter Twelve

Sickness, Disease & Injuries

It is amazing when I consider how far I have come from the days of drive-by healing, (as I called them) to The Altar of Love. I would, and still do, just approach people anywhere and everywhere and ask if I can pray for them. At first I looked for people who had visible physical injuries, but I soon learned that people have all kinds of needs in their personal and professional lives, as well, so I began asking all kinds of people randomly, or as the Holy Spirit led me.

As I was leaving the gym one day, I noticed a man walking towards me. He was strong, confidant, and like most guys, not making eye contact. Truly heterosexual men are funny; at best we'll give a stranger a nod of acknowledgement. At about 20 feet away, I hear the Holy Spirit say, **_Pray for him._** Crud...no, I don't want to bother him, and I can clearly see he doesn't want to be bothered, because he's got that, "don't mess with me" look about him. So, I ignored him, walked right on by, and about 20 feet after I passed him I heard, **_PRAY FOR HIM!_** loud and clear like I had before. It felt like I was being sternly chastised, so I stopped, turned around and shouted, "Hey"! He turned around and with all his male bravado said, "What?" His defenses were up and he seemed a bit annoyed with me, but nothing major. "You need prayer for something very important," I said. Immediately, all his defenses went down, and his whole demeanor changed. He said, "Oh yeah I do. I just found out they diagnosed my brother with lung cancer." We stood right there in the middle of the gym parking lot, and I began to pray for his brother, taking Authority over the spirit of cancer and commanding it to bow to the name of Jesus.

The following day, I had several people tell me they saw me praying for someone in the parking lot and asked if I would pray for them, as well. They all got healed. The real testimony came a few weeks later when I got a text from him saying the cancer was completely gone. Everybody knows that lung cancer never just goes away. It is a death sentence. Nobody ever lives through lung cancer, but with God's help, they can.

I feel like I have five or six different ministries. The gym is certainly a ministry. I pray for people there all the time. At my gym location, is where I do most of my shopping and that is a ministry, as well. I pray for clerks, shoppers, pretty much anybody that the Holy Spirit tells me to. I have a YouTube ministry with a few thousand subscribers. I preach occasionally at my church when called upon, and often pray for people that are just walking by my business. At work, I take many phone calls from people trying to sell me anything from credit card processing to insurance and many times I will take that opportunity to pray for them and they get healed.

One day, I called the dentist where my daughter was getting some work done and I wanted to pay for her service over the phone. I sensed the young girl I was talking to had a back injury and she confirmed that she was in terrible pain from an injury she suffered 10 years ago. She is now in her mid 20's and has been in severe pain for a decade. I asked her if she knew Jesus and she said that she did. I told her to take her right hand and put it on her back and before I even said a word she began telling me that her hand was on fire and it was spreading throughout her entire body. We spoke to the injury and commanded it to be healed, in the name of Jesus.

Now, when I do this, I never like to do it for them. I make them say it with me, that way they are learning how to do it, as well. I made her repeat after me, "In the name of Jesus, I speak life into my back, I command all my disks to align, I command the space between my disks to return to normal, I command all the ligaments, tendons, muscles and nerves to be healed and restored to normal, I command my spine to align and I command all pain to go, in Jesus name. I loose strength, flexibility and mobility in Jesus name." When we finished, she said she needed to leave the phone to run the charge, so I asked her to do something she normally could not do without pain, and report back to me. She came back about a minute later and said she just picked up a super heavy file box, that she could not pick up earlier that day, but now she did it with ease and with no pain.

I really didn't want to make this section all about testimonies, but every testimony of healing had a new and different lesson in it for me, so we'll just see where it takes us. Anyway, let's get back to The Altar of Love process. After casting off all the demonic vermin from occult activity, sexual sin, and witchcraft like behavior, I focus on the physical ailments last, because many of them are there because of the demonic spirits, and once the spirits are gone, so are the symptoms, many times. This is where it gets interesting. Sometimes the demons can't wait to leave and other times they hold on for dear life. When I inquired of the Father regarding this, he showed me that they, too, had personalities and some were cowardly and others were stubborn. Some are smart and leave before I get to ripping them to pieces, but others must be stupid and try to hang on at all costs, and to their own peril they get decapitated and castrated in the process.

It is important to follow the lists, but it is not uncommon for people to remember other sin while we are in the process. If they think of something else, just add it to the end of the list or slide it in where you think it belongs. Address sicknesses and diseases first, and physical injuries last. Address one sickness/disease at a time, then focus on each symptom individually, as well.

Let's use the case below as an example. I addressed the Fibromyalgia first. I assumed Authority over it, I commanded it to bow to the name of Jesus, I commanded it to come out, I had it ripped apart and sent to the pit of Hell, never to be rejoined and never to return. Next I addressed each symptom of Fibromyalgia like it was a separate entity, because they are. I took Authority over weakness, I bound it, removed it, shred it and cast it to Hell, and I did that for each and every symptom.

When I am done with every disease and every symptom, then I begin loosing whatever is needed to fill the void. I loosed strength and might in place of weakness. I loosed energy and endurance in place of fatigue. For the sore muscles, I loosed healing, restoration and peace. For skin sensitivity, I loosed restoration and healing of the nerve endings, commanding any inflammation to go and peace to come, in Jesus name. For numbness I loosed restoration in the nerve endings and renewed sensitivity in fingers and toes. In place of pain, I loosed peace, joy, hope, grace and mercy.

Example of actual case:

Fibromyalgia
Weakness
Fatigue

Muscle soreness

Skin sensitivity

Numbness in fingers and toes

Pain

Arthritis

Knees

Elbows

Hands

Neck

Pain

Multiple Sclerosis

Brain fogginess, difficulty concentrating, memory, attention

Lesions on brain

Muscle pain

Muscle weakness

Tingling, numbness

Fatigue

Balance and coordination

Vision loss

Pain

Every disease must be spoken to and every symptom addressed. Speak to it as if it is a person under your Authority. The physical ailments alone took me the better part of an hour and a half to get through, so the entire case was almost four hours. Before I jump in and begin taking Authority and speaking to these things, I like to go through them in my head first and develop a strategy. I'm not just flying by the seat of my pants here. It's very serious and these people are in severe pain. I consider each sickness and every symptom and I consider how I will bind it and what I will loose in its absence. I have them read me their lists, and as they do, I write my own list, as well. On my list, I am making notes on how I will bind and what I will loose. I am, totally, committed to the case and I've never given up on one yet, and I have never come across one that God could not handle. I've been frustrated and even bewildered at times, but God always shows up if I stay with it. I've been tempted to leave the battlefield early once or twice, but I'm not a quitter and the competitor always comes out of me.

Honesty and full cooperation is imperative. Sometimes they are embarrassed to tell me everything, and I get it, I do, but if we leave anything out, something will stay. If it is spiritual, and we take its Authority away, it must leave, so if it doesn't leave then we missed something. We must have left something out as in the case with the woman and the ouija board. Sometimes, the Father wants to teach them something, but we'll discuss this later.

Physical Injuries

Physical injuries are a completely different animal than spiritual diseases. These are not so cut-and-dry. Watching legs grow before your eyes and bones crack and snap into place will startle and shock even mature believers. For over a year, I suffered with a debilitating hip injury. When I began the healing ministry, I was speaking to my hip daily, but it only got worse. All around me people are getting healed, but not me, I was in agony by the end of each day. While complaining to the Father about it one day, I clearly heard the Holy Spirit say, **_When are you going to trust me?_** So from that day on, my attitude changed. I no longer cared whether or not how, where or when it would happen, I just believed it would and continued to speak to it daily.

Faith is not the Issue

If you have faith the size of a mustard seed, you can say to this mulberry tree, 'Be uprooted and planted in the sea' it will obey you. Luke 17:6

The point behind this verse is in the conditional statement, *If you have faith the size of a mustard seed..* He's not directing us to focus on the seed itself, but on the size of the mustard seed. If anyone has seen a mustard seed, they are smaller than a sesame seed. They are so small, in fact, they look like a speck of dust. The point is, all you need to perform signs and wonders is faith the size of a mustard seed, and anything less than that would be none at all.

Considering the fact that the Word says that God has given each of us a measure of faith, and consider the fact that God never gives anything that is insufficient to do the job properly. Everybody has, at the very least, faith the size of a mustard seed. Therefore, everyone can perform signs, wonders and miracles. Don't ever say you don't have enough faith. That would be a lie from Satan, so don't fall for it. If God has given you a measure of faith, you can bet it's exactly what you need to get the job done.

The very same day I was praying for the really pretty woman at the gym, the one with endometriosis, I noticed a guy listening on to our prayer. Thinking he needed prayer, I asked him later if he needed anything. He didn't, but just wanted to say that he overheard the entire conversation and he acknowledged that the woman was definitely healed and that she must have had great faith.

I tried to tell him that her faith had nothing to do with it at all, and the reason I know this is because the Lord taught it to me several different ways. One way I knew was because he had me pray over many people and not say a word, so that they had no idea what I was doing and they still got healed. Afterwards, when they asked me how I did it, that's when I would tell them I did it in the name of Jesus. Another way He confirmed it was when I prayed for unbelievers and atheists and they got healed. How much faith do they have? None, so how did they get healed if faith was the determining factor? It's not. We are nothing more than a conduit between the Holy Spirit and the person in need. We are the extension cord between the electrical outlet and the appliance.

The man argued with me and incorrectly quoted the verse regarding Jesus not doing many miracles in his home town, because of their unbelief. "That is not what that verse is saying," I replied. "It is saying that their unbelief would not allow Him to do the miracles, because they wouldn't let him pray for anyone. They were mocking Him as a bastard child. There is no record of Jesus praying for someone and them not getting healed." He disagreed with me, so I said, "Ok, I'll show you," and I walked off. As I was walking off, I thought to myself, What have you just done? What do you mean, I'll show you? What will you show him, Father? What have you gotten me into? From there, I walked only a few feet away to an area designated as the abdominal area and as I sat down, a young woman passed by me and I heard the Holy Spirit say, *Her*, so I said, "Hey you," and she stopped and looked at me.

You need to understand, my momma didn't raise a fool. That is not me. I don't talk to people like that, especially not women. I am polite and respectful, but apparently, I'm not able to control the words coming out of my mouth this day. She's pointing at herself as if to say, "Me?" and I say, "Yeah, come here, kneel down in front of me," as I'm sitting on the ground with both of my legs straight in front of me. And that, I would never do, I am never going to tell a woman to kneel down in front of me, ever. So, now I know it's not me, but that's not the best part. The crazy thing is... she does it. This woman, actually, walks over, kneels in front of my feet and I ask her if I have one leg longer than the other. She said that my left leg was about one and one-half inches shorter than my right leg. You recall me saying that my left hip had been bothering me, so I told her to pick up my feet and tell my left leg to come out.

She picks up my feet, with one heel in each hand, looks at me puzzled and says, "Say, what?" I said, "Just repeat after me. Say in the name of Jesus, left leg come out," but she's looking at me like I'm nuts, so I have to do it step-by-step this time. I told her, "Say left leg," she says, "Left leg," I said, "Say, come out," she said, "Come out," and when she did, my left hip popped so loudly that it sounded like a home run hit. It jerked violently in her hand and the thing started moving out.

The girl freaked out, dropped my feet, stumbled back, and said, "How did you do that?" To which I said, "I didn't honey. You did." The look on her face was complete bewilderment, because she doesn't know up from down at this point. Then she said, "How did I do that?" and I said, "Jesus. You did that with the power of Jesus. Do you know Jesus?" She looked at me and said, "No." She did not know Jesus. We're standing up now and she asked me if I would tell her about this Jesus, and I said I would tell her, but before I do, I'm going to show her again just how awesome Jesus is. Not knowing how I knew, I told her that her left rotator cuff was torn. She confirmed that it had been injured for several months, that she was in bad pain, and could not lift her arm above her shoulder.

I took her left hand in my left hand and put my right hand on her shoulder and commanded the rotator cuff to be healed, in the name of Jesus. I commanded the ligaments, the tendons, the muscles, and the nerves to be restored. I commanded the veins to deliver oxygen rich blood to the affected are, so that it may come alive. I commanded it to be made whole and I commanded all the pain to go, in Jesus name. Then I talked to her for a few seconds, because this is a natural occurrence of a supernatural source. It's not like magic and poof, it just happens, but the muscles start to repair, the ligaments stretch and reattach, the nerves come alive, the blood begins to flow and all of it takes a few seconds, so I distracted her.

I, usually, ask questions like how did you hurt it, how long was it hurt, but the most important question is, on a scale of one to ten, what is your pain level, because people need a way to measure the results. After some small talk, I told her to lift her arm up and she lifts it straight up over her head without any pain, whatsoever. Now, she's freaking out and begging me to tell her about this Jesus, so I do and she receives Him as her Lord. Then I asked her if she would share her story with someone and she promised she would.

We walked over to the man that was arguing with me about faith and she told him what happened and he said to her, "So, you did not know Jesus before you got healed?" "No," she replied. Then he said, "So you didn't have faith?" To which she said, "How could I have faith in someone I didn't know?" Then she turned and walked away. As incredible as that testimony is, what I thought was most profound was the fact that she lived her whole life and had never even heard of Jesus. Granted, she had an accent, but it was very light, so she had to be in America for at least 15 years, and no one ever told her about Jesus. How is that possible?

This thing called healing, it's not just for special people with a special gift. It's for Children of God, who know they are Children and walk in Authority. It's not arrogance, but it's definitely a confidence like nothing the world can offer or match. It's Superman in a world without kryptonite. I always thought about it like this: the healing gives a perfect opportunity to minister Jesus to someone, because how are they going to argue with the fact that their torn ACL is no longer torn, or all the pain in their back is now gone? An atheist becomes an instant believer when miracles happen. Later, I saw this verse in Acts:

Lord, enable Your servants to speak Your word with complete boldness, as You stretch out Your hand to heal and perform signs and wonders through the name of Your holy servant. Jesus. Acts 4:30

The healing and the miracles give us the confidence and the opening to preach the Word with more boldness. How bold would you become if you saw miracles when you prayed for people? And not just healing miracles, he's talking about signs and wonders, as well.

These signs will follow all who believe in my name; they will cast out demons, they will speak in new tongues... they will lay their hands on the sick, and they will recover. Mark 16:17

Jesus said that these signs would follow all who believe, not just some, not a few, ALL, and ALL means ALL. If you look up the meaning of 'all' in the Greek, it means all. Not some, ALL. Everyone who believes in Jesus has the potential already inside them. So, why do so few people do it? Because most so-called Christians don't know who they really are and what their Authority is. Those are the two things keeping people from walking like Jesus.

I encourage you today, learn who you are and what you are. Learn to control your tongue. But most importantly, learn to walk in Love. Love everybody, as Jesus loves you.

Physical Injuries & The Spiritual Collide

In the aftermath of the severe flooding due to Hurricane Harvey, I needed to rent a car for a few days. While I approached the counter, the Holy Spirit told me I needed to pray for a certain woman seated in the lobby. She was on the phone at the time so, I figured I'd wait for a more opportune time. As I was being helped by this sweet woman, I felt the urge to lean forward and say, "It's time to go home. Get your affairs in order, because time as you know it is up...it's time to go home." She immediately stopped typing, pushed herself away from her computer and said, "Tell me more."

I told her about my dream of being raptured and how God told me to tell people to come out of the world and come home to their first love. She began asking more and more questions and we had church right there in the lobby of a Hertz Rent-a-Car. A few minutes later, my car was ready, so I took the keys and went to leave. As I walked by the lady that needed prayer, I saw she was still on the phone, so I just left. I got in the car, which was not a car, but a minivan, started it up, put on my seat belt and put it in gear and thought, "Oh heck no, I don't want to drive a minivan. I wanted a car. I reserved a car." I put it back in park, unhooked my seat belt, turned off the engine and proceeded to go back and ask for a car.

As I did, I said a quick prayer for the favor of God to surround me like a shield, so I can get a car. I went to the counter, politely made my request and waited, while they went to check and see if one was available. That's when I noticed the woman who needed prayer was off the phone. I walked over, sat next to her and said, "You have an injury and are in need of prayer." Now this is the weird part and it has happened on more than a few occasions. She said no. Now, I know for a fact that she does, because I heard it, so I started to chat with her while I waited for my car. When I asked why she was there, she said she had been in a car accident nine months earlier, but was still fighting with her insurance over the claim and they had not yet replaced her car.

I asked her if she had any injuries as a result of the accident, and she said that her back was in terrible pain. I chuckled, and asked her why she said she didn't have an injury, when she did. She was a bit embarrassed and didn't have a response. I told her that I represented Jesus and if He told me to pray for her, He was going to heal her. That got her excited, because this woman was a Holy Ghost believer as evidenced by her response to me. I asked her a few questions about her pain...

243

where was it located, how severe was it on a scale from one to ten, and such. I do that, so I know what to speak to and what am I taking Authority over, because if she submits to my prayer, she is submitting to my Authority.

When I finished praying over her back, and let me clarify for a second, what I mean when I say that I prayed over her. As in Mark 11:23 & 24, taking Authority and prayer are two completely different processes. Taking Authority is just that, taking my God given Authority, commanding and demanding that things heal, that things grow, that bones nit, that muscles heal, that ligaments reattach, that eyes see, that diseases bow to the name of Jesus, etc. However, I still consider that to be praying, so if you hear me say I prayed, I may just be taking Authority, instead.

Actual prayer is asking God to intervene in areas that are not under my Authority. Maybe the person would not submit to my Authority and refused prayer, so I prayed for them on my own. Maybe God put them on my heart during my prayer time and the person didn't even know I was praying for them at all. Whatever the case, if I do not have Authority, I will sow the Word of God over the person or situation in prayer, but I do consider both scenarios to be a type of prayer.

I began commanding the back to heal, I spoke to the muscles, the ligaments, the tendons and I'm commanding them to align, to be restored, to be healed, and to be strengthened. Next, I'm speaking to her spine to align, to the vertebrae to be healed, to the disks and the space between the disks to be healed, restored, and repaired. I'm speaking to the nerves to be healed, to be restored, to come alive in the name of Jesus. After taking

Authority over all the physical injuries, I speak to pain and command it to go, in the name of Jesus.

I am, continually, tossing around the name of Jesus when I do any kind of prayer or Authority healing. Lastly, I loosed flexibility, strength, mobility, and peace upon her. When I finished praying for her, I asked her to do something she could not. She said she could not bend over from a standing position since the accident, so she stood up, bent over and touched her toes with ease. Excited, she sat back down and said, "But my neck still hurts." This happens a lot and what I learned was that if there is still pain left, if some symptoms are not gone, do not give up. I have prayed for people that saw their pain go from a ten to a five, from five to three, from three to one, and from a one to zero. Then I saw this passage in Mark 8.

So He took the blind man by the hand and led him out of the village. Then He spit on the man's eyes and placed His hands on him. Can you see anything? He asked. The man looked up and said, I can see the people, but they look like trees walking around. Once again Jesus placed His hands on the man's eyes, and when he opened them his sight was restored, and he could see everything clearly. Mark 8:23-25

Notice how the man could see after the first time Jesus placed His hands on his eyes, but not well, so Jesus did it again and he saw perfectly. I don't know why. He has not told me yet. All I know is that I stay with it till it's all gone, or until no more progress is made, whatsoever.

Going back to the woman in the car rental shop, I put my hand on her neck and as I began to pray, I saw her accident happen in front of me. It was really violent and when the crash occurred, the spirit that was assigned to her used that opportunity to enter her. I heard it called by name. It was a spirit of trauma. It uses traumatic situations to enter people, attaches to the actual physical injury and never lets go of it. That is why people that get into a car accident are still suffering back and neck injuries years later even though there are no physical explanations for their pain. The x-rays show nothing, but the pain is very real.

I stopped and told her what I saw and proceeded to bind and cast out the spirit of trauma, and immediately she felt it go. She stood right up with a spring in her step that she did not have before and began dancing all over the lobby. I even had her give a testimony on my YouTube channel and posted it for everyone to see. She was so happy and so grateful and asked if I would pray for other people she loved. Of course, I said yes and gave her my number. She called me a day later and asked me to take down the YouTube video upon request from her lawyer due to the ongoing case. I did and prayed that it would not affect her healing. I was afraid it might come back as she was going forward with suing the insurance company for the injuries that were now healed. I can't imaging God is going to be okay with insurance fraud.

The lesson here was that Satan will use an actual physical injury to usher in a demonic spirit. The trauma of the accident gave opportunity to the spirit to enter and she never noticed it, because the injuries were real. However, sore muscles heal over time, inflammation goes away and the human body heals itself. Within a few months, everything should have been healed and the pain should have subsided, but this is where the demonic spirit took over and that pain would have stayed for the remainder of her life until someone took Authority over it.

Because she had not given her Authority away by virtue of sinful behavior, she didn't need to repent or confess, but only take Authority. I'm of the opinion that she will be dealing with it again and this time she will need to repent for the fraud first. And just in case you are wondering, I did warn her that such a thing may happen, if she goes forward with the case.

Why Things Do Not Get Healed

There are times when not everything gets healed and I learned over time and experience that God has very specific purposes for leaving some things behind. Remember that little church that I said I was hiding out in? Well, God did a total miracle the second to the last time I attended there. First, as I walked up to the front door, I was approached by my brother who was serving as a greeter that day. He asked if I would pray for a man who was sitting in the lobby with a bad back injury. I went in, found the guy, had him sit in a chair and extend his legs to which we saw he had one that was several inches shorter than the other. I spoke to the leg and it grew out, had him stand, spoke to his back and he was healed.

Another gentleman who was watching, asked for prayer for his back, because it was hurt, as well. He, too, had a short leg and he, too, got healed. I know there was a third one, but I can't remember it offhand. Anyway, after the service they have the elders go to the front to pray for people. The lights were low and the praise and worship team was playing soft music, when I heard the Holy Spirit tell me to pray for one of the prayer partners. I just ignored it, so He said it again and now I'm just arguing with Him. *Go pray for him*, He says. "No, he's the prayer partner, he doesn't need prayer. He's the one doing the praying not being prayed for, that's just weird. What am I supposed to do, just go ask him what he needs prayer for?"

The Holy Spirit actually responded, *Just go tell him he needs prayer.* As I sheepishly move down the aisle and around the seats towards him, my carnal mind kicks in and proceeds to dissuade me from doing what I was told to do. The carnal mind is a very real and very persuasive opposition to the spiritual mind. My carnal mind was telling me that I was going to embarrass myself. It was telling me that that what I was planning on doing was stupid. I didn't really hear from the Holy Spirit. It had to be my own thoughts and I was making all this up.

This was actually a very effective tactic at this time, because I was still relatively new at all this, so it was really messing with me, but I went to him anyway. As we came together, he asked me what I needed prayer for and I leaned in to his right ear and said, "I don't. You do. What did you injure this week?" I could tell it caught him off guard, but he responded and said he totally blew out his back trying to lift something heavy. He was in excruciating pain, just standing there. Now, I'm just embarrassed for being reluctant.

At this time we are as close as two guys will ever get. I told you before, we're weird like that. Our right hands are clenched between us. That's the safe space, lol, but I move in as close as I can get to him, so I can put my left hand on his back as I begin to speak to it with Authority. Immediately, his back starts cracking and popping these loud pops, like when you crack your knuckles, but way louder. It started at the bottom and went up his spine, one vertebrae at a time, and when it was done, he was standing four inches taller.

This is where it got weird, because neither one of us moved. We were as close as two guys can get and we are not leaving this place, because the presence of Holy Spirit was so thick, you could cut it with a knife. It was a type of energy field, like a feeling of light, energy, and life was surging through each of us and neither of us want to leave this place. The awkwardness of the closeness was no longer even a consideration. If you've ever felt this presence then you know what I'm trying to describe, but there just are not words to adequately explain it. It's like we were enveloped in a cocoon of the Holy Ghost and nothing else in the world mattered. No thought could enter to distract my mind and there was no pain or negative emotion or anything, but pure love and light and life. So there we are, two guys hugging for several minutes and we're not leaving this place.

Suddenly, I noticed the pastor's stare of disapproval, because he wanted to end the service, and we were still left standing at The Altar. It didn't matter to us, we weren't going anywhere. Finally, I said to him, "Dude, do you feel it too?" "Of course," is all he said. I said, "If it's all the same with you, it's okay with me if we just stay here." To which he replied, "I told myself that if you tried to leave, I wasn't going to let you go." To which I laughed and I want to say that we stayed like that for another 5 minutes before the Spirit finally faded away.

I learned a valuable lesson that day about the carnal mind. Don't listen to it. We have a spiritual mind, the mind of Christ, that talks to us and influences us to do the Will of the Father. The carnal mind is controlled and manipulated by demonic spirits to stop you from doing your Father's Will and do theirs instead. It's an epic battle that never ends...EVER! Over time you will get better at recognizing the carnal mind, but the key is to tell it to SHUT UP! Do not listen to it or else it will talk you out of doing your Father's Will every time. He will come up with some reason why you should not approach someone for prayer: You're going to embarrass yourself, they don't want to be bothered, what if nothing happens, there's not enough time, do it later, you'll see them again, what if they don't believe you, etc.

The carnal mind is probably the most difficult part of the entire process of spontaneous prayer, and you have to get stiff necked with it and tell it to shut up. Every time I go to pray for somebody, my carnal mind tries to talk me out of it, EVERY TIME, so don't think that I've got some special spirit inside me that isn't nervous or a bit timid or insecure, because I feel all those emotions, but I've learned to ignore them. For the most part, it's still a daily battle and I venture to say, it's probably the most difficult part of all.

The next Sunday, after the service, I was in the lobby about to leave when I feel the Holy Spirit telling me not to go. There is some time between the ending of the first sermon and the beginning of the second one. You have people coming and going now and I am just standing up against the wall near the entrance waiting for a prompting of the Holy Spirit. Finally, I see a young man, 30-ish, who is limping terribly. Then I notice his arm is deformed and his whole left side is underdeveloped.

Guess what happened next? The Holy Spirit said, **Him**, but my carnal mind kicked into high gear... You really do not think you have the power or authority or faith to heal that guy, just look at those injuries. You will make an utter fool of yourself if you even try. People will be talking about you, mocking you for trying to be some kind of faith healer. Besides, you know they don't believe in healing here. The Holy Spirit is never here... you know that. This was the dumbest thing he could've considered, because the Holy Spirit just showed up big time the week before.

I asked him if he would let me pray for him and he eagerly agreed. Trying not to make a show out of it, we quietly sat down in two chairs against a wall, but we are still in the main part of the lobby. I asked what the issue was and he said he was in a car accident when he was twelve and the injuries he sustained damaged his growth plates and stunted the development of the entire left side of his body. He described the actual medical condition, which I can't remember now, but I know that it was bad. He had absolutely no development in his biceps, triceps, forearm, or deltoid muscles. They were completely atrophied from non-use. His leg was somewhat developed, because he could walk, but not very well.

At this point, I'm trying to develop a strategy and determine what to do first, because I can tell this is going to be a huge healing session. I decided to begin with his legs. I lift them up to find his left leg is at least six inches shorter than his right. It grows out completely and people are starting to gather around. I begin speaking to his leg muscles, his quadriceps, his hamstrings, and his calf muscles. They all begin to grow, develop, and strengthen. I spoke to his tendons and ligaments to lengthen and strengthen, and they do. I have him get up and walk and he's walking normal for the first time in 18 years.

He's really excited now and comes back and says, "Do my arm, do my arm." I start speaking to his arm, which did not straighten, because the tendons and ligaments had shrunk from inactivity. Everything starts growing and developing, and suddenly, he has strength in his biceps and triceps. I make him curl his arm upward, while I push down and he's strong now. I'm having to use a lot of strength to give him resistance, because the muscles are so developed. He had the same results with his triceps and shoulder muscles. They were all restored to full strength.

Lastly, I worked on his left hand, which was much smaller than his right hand. His left fingers were about a full inch shorter than the right ones and he lacked strength in his grip, because his forearm muscles were not developed. I start speaking to his muscles, his ligaments, his tendons, his bones, his joints, his nerves, and everything to grow, in the name of Jesus. First, his grip came back and he started squeezing my finger hard, but I wasn't seeing growth in the length of his fingers, only the strength. I took his index finger at the base and began pulling and sliding upward towards the nail, repeatedly demanding that it grow. After a minute or two, we lined up his palms and the index finger had grown out completely. It was the exact same size as the right one.

At this point, we're both freaking out, because this is way cool and I noticed the associate pastor giving me the evil eye from across the room, but too bad, because the Holy Spirit was on a mission. I start grabbing each finger one-by-one and pulling it from the bottom to the top, over and over, as I'm commanding each one of them to grow, in the name of Jesus. After about 10 minutes, we lined up his palms and every finger had grown to the perfect size except his ring finger. So, I go back to it and spend 10 more minutes commanding and demanding, and every time we lined up his palms... nothing. It remained ¼ inch shorter than his right. Mind you, it was an inch shorter, and now, it's only a quarter inch, but it frustrated me. Although I worked on it for half an hour, it never grew another centimeter.

The following day, I received a word from one of my YouTube subscribers regarding the situation, as I had posted the testimony. It was our understanding that the Lord wanted it to remain shorter and He chose his ring finger, because he wanted it to be a daily reminder of the awesome miracle he received when he puts on his wedding ring.

He Wants You to Practice

Due to the ugly looks I got from the associate pastor, and the prompting of the Holy Spirit, that was the last time I attended that church. After the Lord taught me The Altar of Love, I began to bring people through sessions, and I found one common theme, one thing that everyone had upon completion. They all had at least one ache, one little pain, one little something that would not go away. It was always something that was small in significance, as compared to all the other things they were dealing with, but significant enough that it needed to be dealt with. After dealing with one such case, the Holy Spirit brought back to my remembrance the man with the one short finger. In my spirit I felt the Holy Spirit telling me that these people needed something to stay if they were going to get and stay free. Then He showed me why.

This process is just that, a process, and a daunting one at that. Most people are not going to be naturally adapt at it. It is a huge undertaking that requires a bit of practice. That is one of the reasons why I encourage people to teach it, as soon as, they are done doing it, because teaching something is the best way to learn it. Knowing that many are called, but few take the challenge, they need another way to learn it. If all the ailments go, they will never do it again. If something should arise a year from now, they won't remember how we did it and will be back to their old self. Authority must be assumed continually, day after day, week after week, month after month for the rest of your life. Because Authority not assumed, is given to the enemy. I'm sorry, but that's how the Kingdom of God works.

In Jesus' time, they lived without creature comforts. They walked for miles every day. They put 100 pound jugs of water on their head, walked an hour each way, and may have done it two or three times a day. They cooked on open fires, washed clothes and themselves in the river, and generally worked like dogs from the moment they woke up until the sun went down at night, and it started all over again each day. And I'm probably not even close to knowing how hard it was for them, so when Jesus brought this kingdom principle to them, compared to what they did each day, Authority was a walk in the park. You are just using words. It's not as hard as plowing a field with a stubborn ox. Good gracious, were just speaking words here.

We, on the other hand, have become so spoiled and lazy that taking Authority with our Words is like some unbearable responsibility of a difficult job given to us by an evil taskmaster. It's just words ya'll, it's just words. The only thing we're doing is assuming Authority with the words out of our mouth. It requires us to speak, which we have no problem with, when doing it on behalf of the Devil, as we gossip or slander people, as well as, confessing against ourselves.

Your father loves you so much that He will allow that nagging injury to stay, so that you are forced to either live with it or take Authority over it and speak to it every day, until it goes. It's simply words. Now, go and feed the sheep with your words and Authority.

Chapter Thirteen

The Top of The Altar of Love: Repent, Submit, Obey God, and Preach Repentance

The LORD your God is God, the faithful God who keeps covenant and steadfast love with those who love Him and keep His commandments, to a thousand generations.
Deuteronomy 7:9

He is promising to keep covenant with those who love Him and keep His commandments. It's not an either/or requirement. Here, it's both or nothing.

Jesus Christ is the same yesterday and today and forever.
Hebrews 13:8

God has not changed, nor will He. He remains the same regardless of how we feel about it.

...For it is by grace you have been saved through faith, not of yourselves; it is the gift of God, not by works, so that no man can boast. Eph 2:8

Works - Strong's #2041 (er'-gon) Short Definition: work, labor, action, deed. Implies earning one's salvation by doing good deeds.

... not by works, so that no one can boast. Nobody will be able to stand in Heaven and brag about what they have done to get there. However, is it works when we keep God's commandments? Certainly not. Keeping God's commandments

is not the same as trying to earn one's salvation by works. Keeping the commandments simply implies obedience.

But Samuel replied, What is more pleasing to the LORD: your burnt offerings and sacrifices or your obedience to his voice? Listen! Obedience is better than sacrifice, and submission is better than offering the fat of rams. 1 Sam. 15:22

Submission - Strong's #7181 Qashab - To listen and obey. We are in submission when we listen and obey the commandments. Not just listen, listen and obey. Rebellion is the exact opposite of submission. When we don't listen and don't obey, we are in rebellion. Satan was in rebellion, and his OSAS doctrine is one of rebellion, because people who buy into it refuse to submit, to listen, and obey the commandments. Why? Because they don't see the need. They're covered by grace, by gosh, and they can do anything they want...NOT! Are you beginning to see the rebellion, the pride, the arrogance?

Bring your worthless offerings no longer, Your incense is an abomination to Me. I cannot endure iniquity. I hate your new moon festivals and your appointed feasts, They have become a burden to Me; Wash yourselves, make yourselves clean; Remove the evil of your deeds from My sight. Cease to do evil, Learn to do good; Seek justice, Reprove the ruthless, Defend the orphan, Plead for the widow. Come now, and let us reason together, says the LORD, Though your sins are as scarlet, The will be as white as snow; Though they are red like crimson, They will be like wool. If you consent and obey, You will eat the best of the land; Isaiah 1:13-19

When I read this, I could feel the heart of the Father pleading with His children to stop their iniquity. He's so fed up with their rebellion that the sacrifices no longer interest Him. He's done with them, their sacrifices are worthless now. All He desires is obedience. That's all He wants from us, that, and a contrite and repentant heart. First He goes through an entire list of offenses, then He offers to wash them white as snow, if they consent and obey, which is basically the same thing as submit and obey.

The Modern Church has been deceived into thinking that works and obedience are synonymous... they're not. If God is the same yesterday, today, and forever, and he demanded obedience then, what makes us think he does not demand it now? Why is it that the very people railing against the mega churches' watered down version of the gospel and it's prosperity message are the same people parroting the OSAS message of the mega churches they rail against?

One thing The Altar of Love taught me was that we are expected to repent, submit, and obey. Obeying God is not works, it's not even a responsibility. It's something we should desire to do, because we love Him. Repentance brings us back to the throne, where we can obtain grace and mercy in our time of need. If we are frequent sinners, repentance brings us back frequently to that throne room, and that's the safest and best place in the world to be. As well, we benefit the most from repentance and forgiveness, because it takes back our Authority and puts us back in the driver's seat. If we love God, we will want to obey Him. Jesus said, *If you love me, keep my commandments.*

If you recall, Jesus rolled all Ten Commandments into two. Love God and love people. Jesus said, *If you hate, it's just as if you murdered, and if you lust, it's just as if you commit adultery.* So, we see here that walking in the commandment of love requires us to walk circumspectly. Understand that the Devil will plant thoughts in your mind, but that is not where sin occurs. Sin occurs when we take Satan's planted thought and meditate upon it within our hearts, plotting and planning it. That is why we are instructed to take every thought into captivity to determine its origin. Is it from God or not? If it is not, we are to cast it down to the obedience of Christ. See, there's that word obedience again.

This is perfectly described in the first chapter of James,

> *But every man is tempted, when he is drawn away by his own desire, and enticed. Then after desire is conceived, it gives birth to sin; and when sin is fully grown, it brings forth death.* James 1:14-15

And this is how it works. Satan knows our weaknesses. He knows exactly what to tempt you with. Remember, He's had a demon assigned to you since birth. He knows exactly what tempts you and what doesn't. What He is offering you is only temporary, however, because in the end, it brings death.

Sin has the exact same effect on us as heroin has on the brain. It is said that the first high is so awesome, because it makes a complete dump of dopamine into the brain causing an unparalleled euphoric experience that the user desperately tries to recreate, but is physically unable to, because the brain cannot recreate that amount of dopamine again. Furthermore, with each use, the dopamine decreases, so that the user is having to use more and more until they finally overdose. Likewise with sin, at first it is exciting and pleasurable, but like heroin, it's end is death. Your Father, on the other hand, is offering you peace, joy, hope, and eternal salvation.

This is not implying that you will die physically, although it may, depending upon what the sin is, but mostly that sin will cause death to the situation, for example, a beautiful marriage destroyed, because of one act of adultery. The impending divorce affects a child, so that they escape to drugs causing a descent into destructive behavior, that leads to a completely different outcome than the way it would have been, without the adulterous affair. Sin brought death to what should have been a beautiful family life.

I call Heaven and earth as witnesses today, that I have offered you life or death, blessings or curses. Choose life so that you and your descendants will live. Deut 30:19

Obedience or sin is a choice. We either choose our Father and what He is offering or we choose the Devil and the death He is offering. Who and what we serve is determined by our choices not by mere words of a sinner's prayer. The Father searches and knows the hearts of man. If a man tells his wife he truly loves her, but is having casual sex, whenever he goes away on business, he does not really love her. Expecting God to overlook our disgusting behavior by claiming that we said a sinner's prayer, is like expecting the wife to forgive and forget her husband's adultery, without a promise of repentance.

Having been caught by his wife, the husband, filled with guilt and remorse, begs and pleads for forgiveness vowing never to do it again. The wife may choose to forgive her husband if she truly loves him, (and knowing that Satan is a very real adversary), and knowing her husband, she believes he is sincere. On the other hand, if his attitude is one of indignance, and there seems to be no remorse or repentance, but he responds with, "It happened. Get over it. Besides, we're married, you can't leave me." She'd be a fool not to divorce him.

Likewise, is the false OSAS doctrine of demons. It implies that we are given a free pass to sin as much and as often as we want, without repercussions and no need for remorse, and that is a lie from Hell.

These people honor Me with their lips, but their hearts are far from Me, in vain do they worship me, teaching as doctrines the commandments of men. Matthew 15:8

This is what I hear the Lord speaking to my heart. Nowhere, in the Bible is the phrase, "Once saved, always saved." It is a doctrine of demons for people who wish to excuse their habitual sin. They have created their own God, breaking the first commandment, and have invented their own gospel to suit their own lustful desires. It is the doctrine of mega churches, designed to tickle the ears of this "do whatever makes you feel good" culture, that is always just looking for an excuse to sin. This doctrine is not consistent with the God of Abraham, the God of Moses or the God of David, and we know He is the same yesterday, today, and forever. A God whose mantra from the beginning has been, is, and will always be: believe, repent, and obey.

In repentance and rest you will be saved, In quietness and trust is your strength. But you were not willing. Isaiah 30:15

Notice, it says, repentance and rest, not either/or.

...And with whom was God angry for forty years? Was it not with those who sinned, whose bodies fell in the wilderness? And to whom did He swear that they would never enter His rest? Was it not to those who disobeyed? So we see that it was because of their unbelief that they were unable to enter their rest. Therefore, let us fear if, while a promise remains of entering His rest, lest anyone of you seem to have come short of it. Heb 3:17-19

Paul is saying that our rest is in Jesus and obedience, not one or the other. Otherwise, why would he tell them *to fear... lest they come short?* To "come short," means they do not make it. Do not make what? Their rest, God's rest, SALVATION, HEAVEN. It was used to describe the Jews' final destination into the promised land and a metaphor for a believer's final destination, Heaven. The Jews that Paul was referring to did not make it to Heaven, because they were not willing to obey. Obedience comes from a willing heart. "But that's the old testament," you say. Yes, but Paul is warning his followers that the same will happen to them, as well, if they do not obey. Think about it, if it was not possible for them to lose salvation, why would Paul tell them to fear, lest they come short?

Let me interject here... it wasn't so much that they disobeyed, but their hearts were hardened towards God in their rebellion. There was no remorse or repentance, much the same as the OSAS, who never feel remorse, and therefore, never repent, because they falsely assume every sin is covered by the blood of Jesus, and they are not entirely wrong. Every sin is covered by the blood of Jesus, BUT ONLY AFTER THEY REPENT AND ASK FORGIVENESS for their sin. Otherwise, it's just sin that piles up into a mountain called, rebellion. Remember, sin brings separation, but repentance brings restoration and develops the relationship, and our Father loves the relationship.

Rest - Strong's #2663 (kat-ap'-ow-sis) Rest, literally, rest attained by the settlement in Canaan. Metaphorically, the heavenly blessedness in which God dwells, and of which, He has promised to make persevering believers in Christ partakers after the toils and trials of life on Earth are ended.

For to us was the gospel preached, as well as, to them: but the word preached did not profit them, not being mixed with faith in them that heard it. For we who have believed enter that rest, as he has said, As I swore in my wrath, They shall not enter my rest. (Who are they? Those who do not mix the Word preached to them with faith/belief. You only do the word you believe. If you will not do that Word you heard preached, you don't believe it. If you don't believe it, you don't have faith in it. No faith, no rest.) *They shall not enter my rest, Therefore, since it remains for some to enter into God's rest, but those who first heard this good news failed to enter because of their disobedience.* Heb 4:2

If there was any doubt to the belief that our salvation was not guaranteed by saying a **sinner's prayer**, this next verse should put them to rest. We know Paul is talking to believers, because he is including himself in the discussion when he says,

If we deliberately go on sinning after we have received the knowledge of the truth, no further sacrifice for sins remains, If we deliberately go on sinning after we have received the

knowledge of the truth, no further sacrifice for sins remains, but only a fearful expectation of judgment and raging fire that will consume all adversaries. How much worse punishment, do you think, will be deserved by the one who has trampled underfoot the Son of God, and has profaned the blood of the covenant by which he was sanctified, and has outraged the Spirit of grace? It is a terrifying thing to fall into the hands of the living God. Hebrews 1026-31

As a believer, and because we should know better than unbelievers, if we sin deliberately and do not repent, there is no sacrifice for our sin. Deliberate sin will send a believer to the Lake of Fire. He, also, makes it sound as if it is an insult to God, one that people should be terrified about.

Not everyone who says to me, 'Lord, Lord,' will enter the kingdom of Heaven, but only the one who does the will of my Father who is in Heaven. Mat 7:21

There is just no way to misinterpret this. These people are calling Jesus Lord. They think they are saved, but they are not. According to Jesus, confessing Him as Lord is not enough; we are expected to do His Will, as well. And what is His will? His Word. Jesus goes on to say,

Many will say to Me on that day, Lord, Lord, did we not prophesy in Your name, and in Your name drive out demons and perform many miracles? Then I will tell them plainly, I never knew you; depart from Me, you workers of lawlessness. Therefore everyone who hears these words of Mine and acts on them is like a wise man who built his house on the rock... Mat 7:22-24

It's here that Jesus tells us exactly why these believers are not welcome into Heaven. Understand that this is not just your typical Christian that is sitting in the back row falling asleep every Sunday. No, this is likely someone in leadership, someone that has prophesied, cast out demons, and healed people. This is the last person that anyone would expect not to make it. Here, Jesus says, *I didn't know you. We didn't have a relationship*, then He called them 'workers of lawlessness.' This is defined as someone that is in habitual sin. They know what they are doing is sin, but they do it anyway. Those deceived by the false grace movement, the once saved-always saved clan are traveling the world to make a convert and turning them into twice the son of Hell they are. "You're saved, so go ahead and do whatever you want, because you're covered by grace." Hogwash! Since when is that ever the character of God? It's not!

Please read this next section very carefully. I read this a hundred times, but this time it came off the page at me in 3D.

> *I say then: Walk in the Spirit, and you shall not fulfill the lust of the flesh. For the flesh lusts against the Spirit, and the Spirit against the flesh; and these are contrary to one another, so that you do not do the things that you wish.*
>
> *But if you are led by the Spirit, you are <u>not</u> under the law. <u>If then, you are fulfilling the lusts of the flesh, you are not led by the spirit and if you are not led by the spirit you are under the law and not grace.</u>*

Do you see it? This is where it got real for me and where God began to show me the how and why. When we are deliberately sinning, we are walking in the flesh, and therefore, we come out from under the grace umbrella. If we walk in the flesh, we are not led by the spirit, and if we are not led by the spirit **we are under the law**, **NOT GRACE**. If we are **led by the spirit**, we are **not under the law,** but if we are **led by the flesh** we are **under the law**. Ok, if being led by the flesh is the culprit that removes our grace covering, what does it mean to be led by the flesh. Paul gives us a perfect example in Galatians 5.

> *Now the works of the flesh are manifest, which are these: Adultery, fornication, perversion, promiscuity, idolatry, witchcraft, hatred, strife, jealousy, wrath, selfishness, divisions, heresies, envy, drunkenness, orgies, and things like these. I warn you, as I warned you before, that those who do such things will not inherit the Kingdom of God.* Gal 5:19-21

How many of us know people who call themselves Christians and are doing many of these? I would venture to say that most, not all, but most people in the OSAS mega churches. I'm sure there are some devout believers sitting in those pews, but not many, because there is a spirit of disobedience swarming in those places. If you submit yourself to that teaching long enough it will have its way with you. All these beautiful brothers and sisters have fallen prey to this false doctrine, thinking they are saved by this false grace message. Remember, Paul said if you are walking in the flesh, as described here, you are no longer under grace, but you are under the law.

The Lord Jesus will come with his mighty angels, In flaming

fire taking vengeance on those who do not know God, and on those who do not obey the gospel of our Lord Jesus Christ. These shall be punished with everlasting destruction from the presence of the Lord and from the glory of His power.
2 Thessalonians 1:8-9

Paul is making a clear distinction between unbelievers and believers when he says, *those who do not know God, and on those who do not obey the gospel.* Remember, the word "know," implies relationship. They had no relationship with God. The second group, supposedly, knew God, but did not obey Him. Both groups will end up in the Lake of Fire. I told you, repent and obey; that is the underlying theme of The Altar of Love. Repentance and forgiveness remove the Authority, so we can expel the beast and by being obedient, we never give Authority away again.

Every tree that does not bear good fruit is cut down and thrown into the fire. Thus, you will recognize them by their fruits. Matt 7:19-20

Every tree! Jesus said that we would be known by our fruit, not by our faith. What does it mean to be recognized by our fruit? Once again, Paul tells us in Gal 5.

But the fruit of the Spirit is love, joy, peace, patience, kindness, goodness, faithfulness, gentleness, and self-control. Against such things there is no Law. Those who belong to Christ Jesus have crucified the flesh with its passions and desires. Gal 5:22-24

We just learned that if we walk in the flesh, we are under the Law, and we learned what walking in the flesh looks like. Now

Paul is describing the opposite; this is what it looks like to walk in the spirit. When we "walk in the spirit," we display the "fruit of the spirit."

Someone asked Him, Lord, will only a few be saved? He replied, Make every effort to enter through the narrow door, because I tell you, many will try to enter and won't be able. After the master of the house gets up and shuts the door, you will stand outside knocking and saying, Lord, open the door for us. But he will reply, I do not know where you are from. Then you will say, We ate and drank with you, and you taught in our streets. But He will say, I tell you, I don't know you or where you're from. Get away from Me, all you workers of unrighteousness! Luke 13:23-28

They try to enter, because they think they are saved. They're calling Jesus Lord, because they think they're saved. Yet, He doesn't know them and once again, He refers to them as 'workers of unrighteousness'... That is, someone that is in habitual sin, without repentance and perfectly describes the OSAS message of the mega churches. Have you ever wondered why they are so MEGA? Because they are tickling the ears with their false grace, do what thou wilt doctrine of demons. All the while, the preacher that teaches repentance has only a handful of devout believers in his congregation.

Enter by the narrow gate; for wide is the gate and broad is the way that leads to destruction, and there are many who go in by it. Because narrow is the gate and difficult is the way which leads to life, and there are few who find it. Matt. 7:13-14

Who do you think Jesus is talking about? The OSAS mega churches are leading millions down the wide path, but the narrow path has only a few devout believers, that love the Lord and desire to keep His commandments, as Jesus said,

If you love me, obey my commandments. John 14:15

This is not rocket science people. We either Love our God and desire to please Him by keeping His commandments or we love the world and please our flesh. We were given free will to choose one or the other; nobody is forcing you to do anything against your will. *But I assure you this, for those who choose the temporary pleasures of this world over a relationship with their Father, there will be weeping and gnashing of teeth.* I know we covered this text earlier, but let's look at it from another angle. Read it slow and pay attention to what it is saying.

Do not love (take no pleasure in) *the world or anything in the world* (what the world offers). *If anyone loves* (desires) *the world, the love of the Father is not in him.* This is not saying that the Father does not love them. It implies that they do not love the Father, because they desire the world more. *For all that is in the world, the lust of the flesh, the lust of the eyes, and the pride of life, is not from the Father but from the world. The world is passing away along with its desires, but whoever does the will of God, remains forever...* 1 John 2:15

What do you think it means when he says. "Whoever does the will of God remains forever?" First, remaining forever implies eternal life in Heaven, and whoever does the will of God gets it. So, what is the will of God? If Jesus said, *If you love me keep my commandments,* and the first commandment was "love God," then it only stands to reason that doing the will of God is keeping His commandments.

Let's see this thing from our Fathers point of view,

Do not prefer Satan or anything in Satan's kingdom. If anyone prefers Satan's kingdom, they do not love the Father. For all that is in Satan's kingdom, he lust of the flesh, the lust of the eyes, and the pride of life, is not from the Father, but from Satan. And Satan is passing away along with his kingdom pleasures, but whoever obeys God, remains forever.

Our loyalty is not based upon what we say in a sinner's prayer, it is based upon who we obey. We can say we love God until we are blue in the face, but if we obey Satan by walking in the lust of the flesh, our disobedience proves our loyalty. If I obey my Father's commandments, my obedience proves my love and my loyalty.

> *No one can serve two masters, for either he will hate the one and love the other, or he will be devoted to the one and despise the other.* Matthew 6:24

Once again, Jesus proves that we cannot live in and for the world and expect everything is going to be hunky-dory when we die. You can't have one foot in the world and one in the Kingdom of God. You have to make a choice. It's God's narrow way or Satan's broad way.

> *I have set before you life and death, blessing and curse. Therefore, choose life.* Deuteronomy 30:19

Make the right choice. Your eternity depends upon it. This is the way I see it. What if the OSAS doctrine is wrong? If they are wrong, they spend eternity in Hell. If I'm wrong, and we are all just saved by grace, then I followed the commandments to the best of my ability and spent a considerable time repenting, praying for forgiveness, and growing closer to my Father. I lost nothing, but they lost everything.

When we consider this is the most important decision of a human's life, there really is no decision at all, is there? It's not like I'm making a decision for a car on a game show and I happened to get it wrong. This is a decision about our eternal life. Is it worth the risk of being wrong? It's like playing Russian Roulette with your salvation. What if you're wrong? Have you ever been wrong before? Have you ever been so certain about something that you would have staked your life on it, only to find out you were wrong?

For it is impossible for those who were once enlightened (saved), and have tasted the Heavenly gift, and have become partakers of the Holy Spirit, and have tasted the good word of God and the powers of the age to come, if they fall away, to renew them again to repentance, since they crucify again for themselves the Son of God, and put Him to an open shame. For the earth which drinks in the rain that often comes upon it, and bears herbs useful for those by whom it is cultivated, receives blessing from God; but if it bears thorns and briers, it is rejected and near to being cursed, whose end is to be burned. Hebrews 6:4

If anyone's name was not found written in the book of life he was thrown into the lake of fire. Revelation 20:15

May they be blotted out of the book of life And may they not be recorded with the righteous. Psalm 69:28

It is possible to be blotted out of the Book of Life.

But the children of the kingdom shall be cast out into outer darkness, there shall be weeping and gnashing of teeth.
Matthew 8:12

The Children of God are cast into outer darkness? Who are the children He is talking about?

But to all who did receive him, who believed in his name, he gave the right to become children of God. John 1:12

If the children of the Kingdom are those that received Christ as Lord and believed upon His name, then why were they thrown in outer darkness?

But the fearful, the unbelieving, the vile, the murderers, the sexually immoral, those who practice magic arts, the idolaters and all liars, they will be consigned to the fiery lake of burning sulfur. This is the second death. Rev 21:8

If your hand causes you to stumble, cut it off. It is better for you to enter life maimed than with two hands to go into Hell, where the fire never goes out. Mark 9:43

If a sinner's prayer alone could keep someone out of Hell, then the above statement was not even necessary.

I could go on and on with dozens more scripture supporting the main point of the new testament, where Jesus and the apostles are saying, *"Repent and obey."* The infamous words of Jesus, *Why do you call me Lord and do not do what I say?* further indicate that a sinner's prayer is not sufficient unto salvation. And those statements alone should be enough to convince anyone that the OSAS mantra is a doctrine of demons designed to lure us into a life of habitual sin and ultimately to Hell.

For where your treasure is, there your heart will be also.
Matthew 6:21

We are not fooling God. He knows what's in our treasure, in our hearts. Repent and go back to your first love, Jesus.

Recap of The Process

Make the lists: (spend time in prayer asking God to reveal things)

- Occult activity

- Sexual sin

- General sin

- Demonic behavior

- Associations with occult persons and/or places, past and

  present

- Sickness / Diseases and all their symptoms (medication)

- Injuries and all their symptoms

- Remove all occult symbols and artifacts from home/work

- Go through Identity, Authority, Power of Words and Love

  lessons

- Repent and confess occult activity/ evict demon spirits

- Repent and confess occult behaviors / evict demon spirits

- Repent and confess sexual sin / evict demon spirits

- Repent and confess general sin / evict demon spirits

Take Authority over all sickness and disease. Command them to bow to the name of Jesus. Send them to the pit of Hell, but not until you have mutilated them. Speak to every symptom of each disease, bind the symptoms, and loose the opposite.

Look for pain, and do it again and again, if necessary.

Do not be surprised if things stay. Anything that does not go immediately, continue to speak to it, taking Authority over it daily. Ask the father if there is any unrepentant sin, anything you may have forgotten.

I have given you authority to trample on snakes and scorpions and to overcome all the power of the enemy; nothing will harm you. Luke 10:19

Special Thanks to...

Lauren and Katerina Rainier of R&R Creative Marketing, for editing the book interior and for designing and creating the book cover.

Christopher Santarose and Trinity Digital Imaging & Design for creating The Altar illustration

Bulabu Publishing

Made in the USA
Middletown, DE
03 May 2019